Maths Matters 2

Prabha Sethy

Collins

Maths Matters 2

Prabha Sethy

Published by Collins India
A division of HarperCollins*Publishers* India Limited
HarperCollins *Publishers*
A-75, Sector 57, Noida, Uttar Pradesh 201301, India
1 London Bridge Street, London, SE1 9GF, United Kingdom
Hazelton Lanes, 55 Avenue Road, Suite 2900, Toronto, Ontario M5R 3L2
and 1995 Markham Road, Scarborough, Ontario M1B 5M8, Canada
25 Ryde Road, Pymble, Sydney, NSW 2073, Australia
195 Broadway, New York, NY 10007, USA

Browse the complete Collins catalogue at **www.collins.in**

First published in 2016
Latest reprint edition 2017

ISBN: 978-93-5136-886-1

Artwork and layout by **Mukesh Technologies Pvt. Ltd.**

Printed and bound in India by Thomson Press India Ltd.

MRP: ₹ 205

Acknowledgements

Cover: WEKWEK, iStockphoto

Title Page: WEKWEK, iStockphoto

Preface

Maths Matters is a series of eight books for Classes 1 to 8. The primary school series follows a universal approach whereas the middle school series is based on the syllabus prescribed by the Inter-State Board for Anglo-Indian Education.

Maths Matters focuses on developing thinking and reasoning skills in students. It enables students to comprehend the application of mathematics in real life. In addition, the coherent and structured approach is valuable for teachers as it helps the lesson flow from one level to the next. Sufficient number of solved examples, exercises and mental maths questions are provided to ensure a holistic grasp of the mathematical thought processes.

Some Key Features

Let's Get Started to revise the concepts learnt earlier

Mental Maths to sharpen the calculation skills and logical reasoning

Hints and Tips for better conceptual understanding

Try These to test student's understanding of the topic covered

Note brings the focus to certain important points

Remember to highlight key points of the concept discussed

Exercise to revise the topics just learnt

Revision Exercise for a well-integrated review of the concepts covered in a chapter

For the Curious Mind to encourage students to think beyond the textual knowledge

Worksheet to reinforce practice with fun exercise

Project to extend the concept learnt to real–life applications

We would like to take this opportunity to thank all the teachers who reviewed the books and provided their valuable feedback which helped in improving the quality of the content.

Any suggestions or constructive criticism from the users are welcome. We shall try to incorporate those in the future editions.

Authors

Key Features

Let's Get Started

To revise the concepts learnt earlier

Let's Get Started

What comes to your mind when you hear
How often do you come across numbers

Numbers are not only used to count, bu
measure and label. For example, numb

Mental Maths

To hone the calculation skills and logical reasoning.

Mental Maths

1. Write the place value of the underlined digits:
   a. <u>9</u>782485 ______
   b. 7<u>6</u>81984

Try These!

To test student's understanding of the concept

Try These!

3 × 2 = ____
5 × 2 = ____
7 × 2 = ____
9 × 2 = ____

Note

To bring the focus to certain important points

Note

Bigger objects may not necessarily be heavier than smaller objects. A lock is heavier than a pencil box

Hints and Tips

To provide hints and tips for better understanding of the concept

Hints and Tips

Distinguish between the terms Cost Price and Actual Cost. Always remember that if overhead expenses are mentioned in the question, then Actual cost = CP + Overhead expenses.

Remember

To highlight key points of the concept discussed

Remember

When we subtract 0 from a number, the value of the number remains the same; it does not decrease.

12345 – 0 = 12345
56789 – 0 = 56789

Exercises

To revise the concepts just learnt

Exercise 9.2

1. A lamp costs ₹835 and a book costs cost?

	H	T	O
Lamp costs			
Book costs			

Thus, both the things cost ₹ ______.

2. Ram has ₹750. Shyam has ₹525. How have than Shyam?

Ram has ₹ ______.
Shyam has ₹ ______.
Thus, Ram has ₹ ______ more

Revision Exercise

At the end of each chapter for a comprehensive review of the concepts

Revision Exercise

1. Choose the correct options.

a. 24 × 1000 =
i. 24 ii. 240 iii. 2,400

b. 56 × 200 =
i. 200 ii. 11,200 iii. 112

c. 569 × 7 =
i. 3,983 ii. 3,987 iii. 5,697

d. 8959 × 9 =
i. 80,630 ii. 80,631 iii. 80,36

e. 72395 × 5 =
i. 3,61,095 ii. 3,61,555 iii.

For the Curious Mind

To encourage students to think beyond the textual knowledge

For the Curious Mind

From the numbers below, find the correct a

355, 500, 710, 183, 940

What number am I?

1. I am between 100 and 200. ______
2. I am 5 more than 350. ______
3. I am greater than 900. ______
4. I am between 490 and 510. ______
5. I am 10 more than 700. ______

Worksheet

To reinforce practice with fun exercise

Worksheet

1. Write the multiplication and division facts for these been done for you.

4 24 6   35 7 5

4 × 6 = 24   ___ × ___ = ___

Summary

To provide the gist of the chapter for quick revision

Summary

1. The word 'per cent' is derived from the Lat meaning 'per hundred' and it is denoted by
2. To convert a percentage to a fraction, divid numeral by 100 and remove the % sign. Th also be changed into the form of a ratio.
3. To convert a ratio or fraction into percent a fraction of hundredths and put the %
4. To convert a percentage into a decima fraction of hundredths and remove

Project

To extend the concept learnt to real – life applications

Project

Look at all the objects in your c plane surfaces and curved sur

Mixed Review

To provide more practice after every few chapters

Mixed Review

1. The pictograph below shows the numbe different days of the week.
If each ● = 1,000 people, then study the pi

Days			
Mon	●	●	◐
Tue	●	●	●
Wed	●	●	●
Thu	●	●	●
Fri	●	●	

Collins DigiSuite is an innovative digital solution for teachers. It contains four modules delivering classroom content that can be used to effectively integrate the teaching and evaluation tools with the coursebooks.

The **E-book** includes animations, interactive exercises and worksheets. The E-book reader also includes interactive teaching tools like pen tool, text highlighter, page zoom, search and bookmark.

The **Test Generator** is a question bank with a variety of questions for effective evaluation. It is an easy-to-use assessment tool for the teachers to create test papers and worksheets.

The **Teacher's Resource** consists of lesson plans, answer keys and teaching techniques for the teachers.

This module has a PDF of the **Collins dictionary** appropriate for each level with all the words and definitions one needs.

Contents

Numbers up to 1000

1

Let's Get Started

Let us revise what we have learned in Class 1.

1. Write the number names of the following numbers.

   a. 8 ____________________ b. 12 ____________________

   c. 39 ____________________ d. 57 ____________________

2. In the pictures given below, encircle the second picture and cross the fifth picture.

3. Fill in the blanks.

   a. ________ comes just before 62. b. ________ comes just after 79.

4. Fill in the blanks.

   a. 35 = ________ tens ________ ones b. 69 = ________ tens ________ ones

5. In 78, the

   a. place value of 7 is ________. b. face value of 7 is ________.

6. Encircle the largest number among the numbers given below.

   13 92 58 7 62

7. Write the following numbers in decreasing order.

   12 89 5 73 61

   ________, ________, ________, ________, ________

Introduction to 3-digit Numbers

In Class 1, we have learned numbers from 1 to 99. If we add 1 to 99, we get

$$99 + 1 = 100.$$

The number name for 100 is 'one hundred'. 100 is a 3-digit number.

Hundreds	Tens	Ones
1	0	0

The digit **0** is at the ones and tens places and **1** is at the hundreds place.

We can write it as:

Hundreds	Tens	Ones
1	0	0

100 is the Smallest 3-digit Number

100 can be represented as a block shown below.

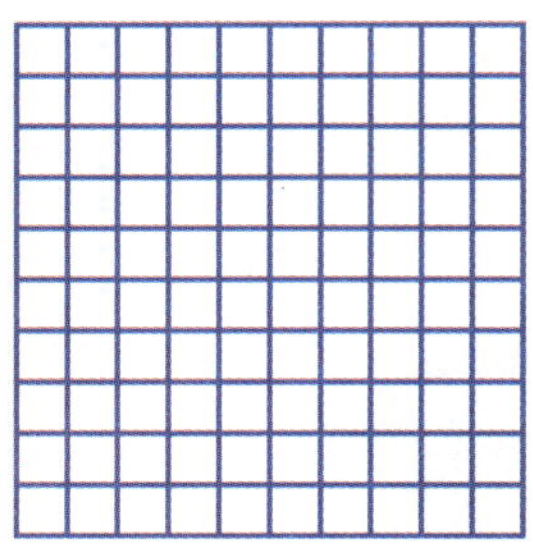

Note

This block has one hundred squares. There are 10 squares in each column.

Counting by Hundreds

Blocks of 100	Numeral	Number Name
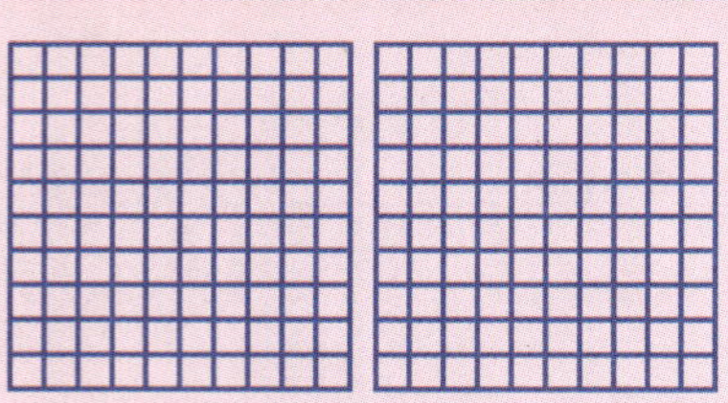	200	Two Hundred
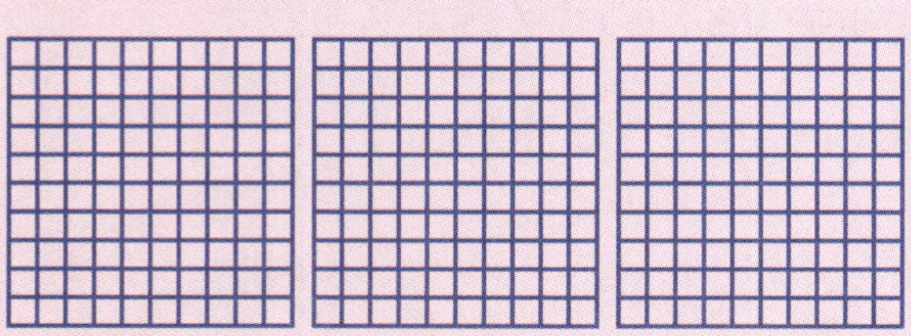	300	Three Hundred
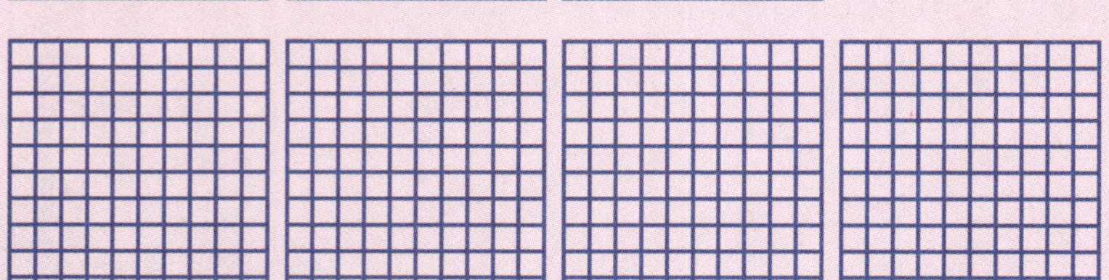	400	Four Hundred

Blocks of 100	Numeral	Number Name
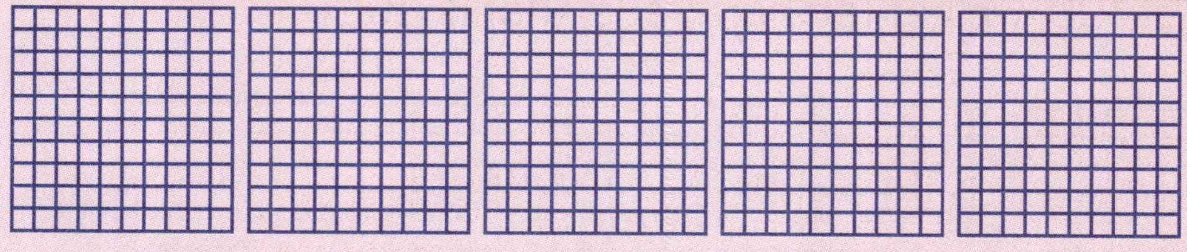	500	Five Hundred
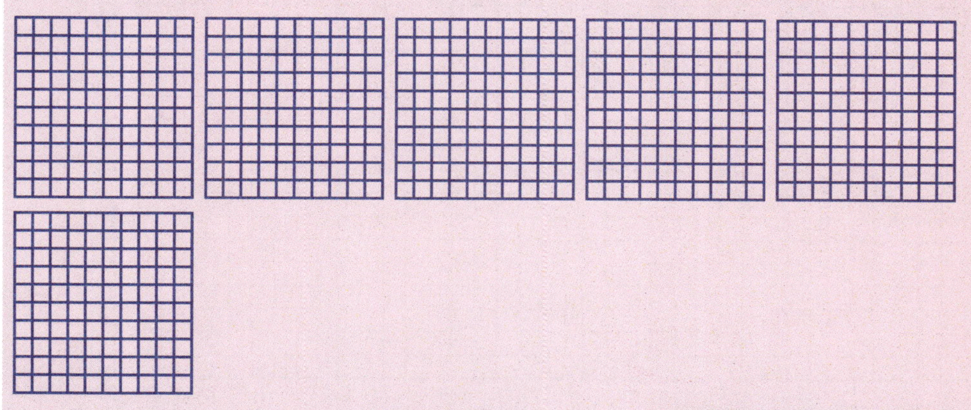	600	Six Hundred
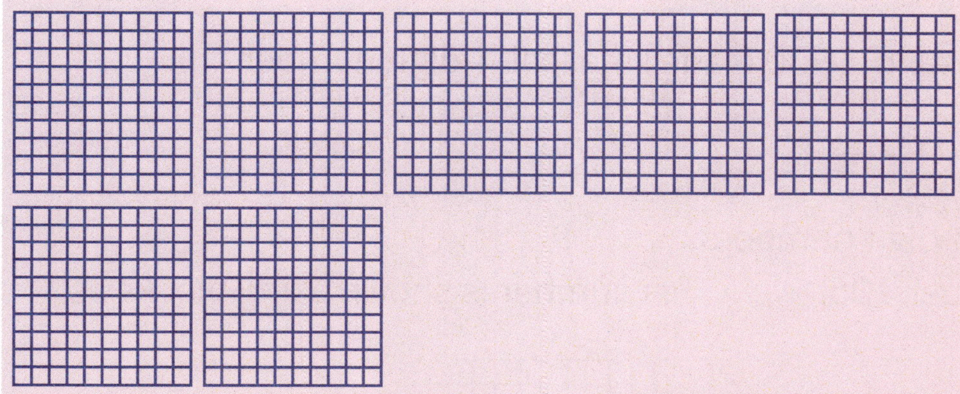	700	Seven Hundred
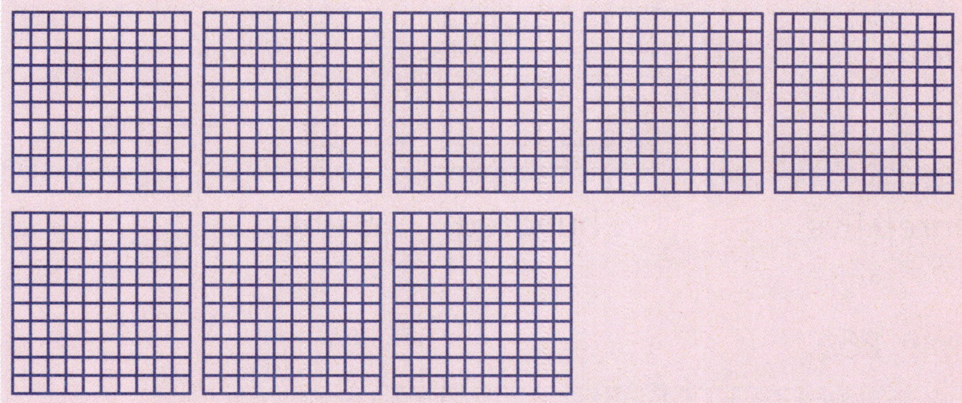	800	Eight Hundred
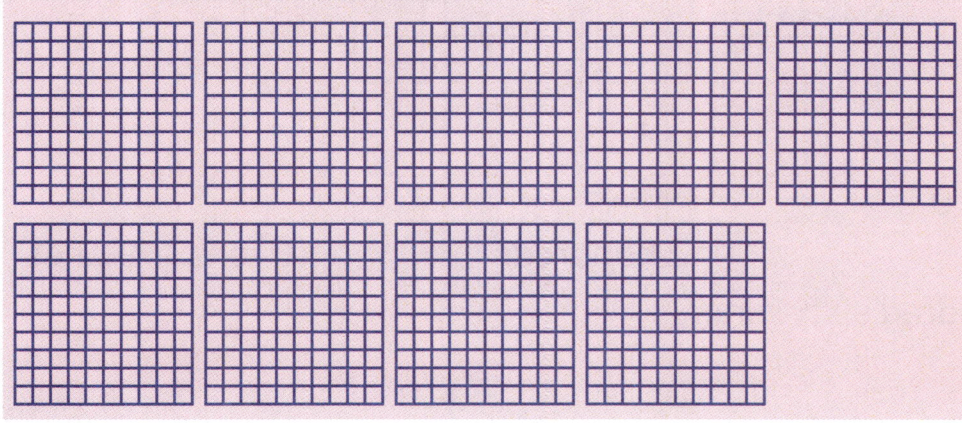	900	Nine Hundred

The Number 1000

If we combine ten blocks of 100, we get ten hundreds, that is, 1000.

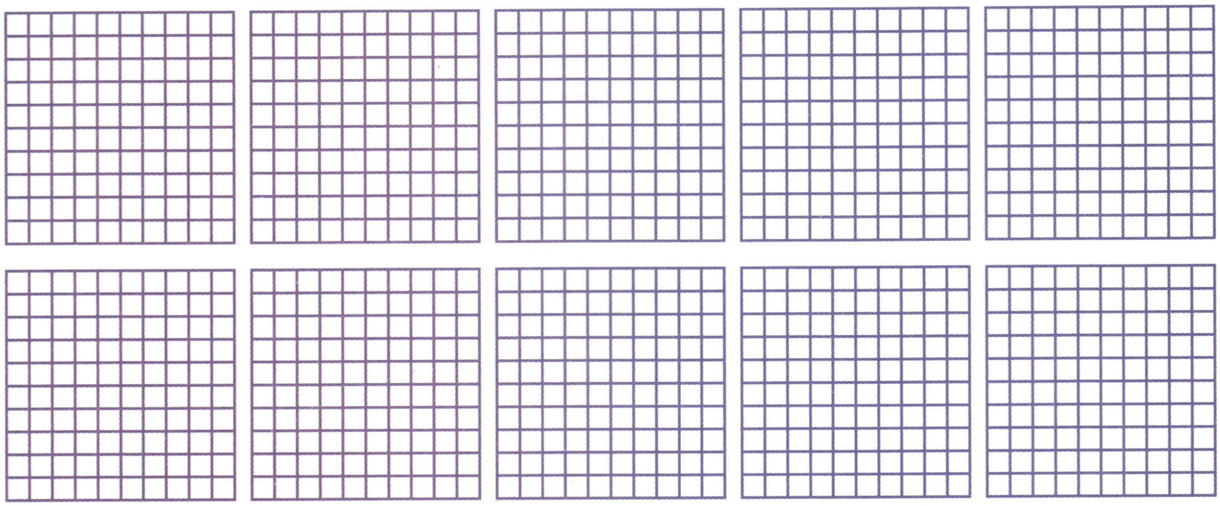

1000 is read as 'one thousand'. 1000 is the smallest 4-digit number.

Forming 3-digit Numbers

Let us learn some more 3-digit numbers.

Let us take a 3-digit number, 105.

We can write it as:

Hundreds	Tens	Ones
1	0	5

Number name = One hundred five

This number is shown using blocks as:

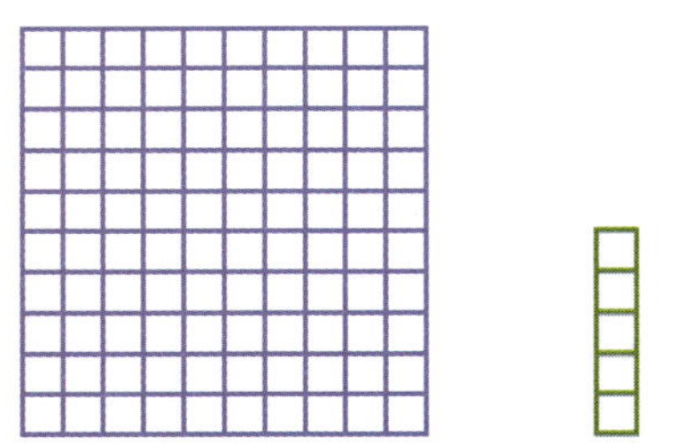

= 105

1 hundred 5 ones

Let us take another example, 269.

We can write it as:

Hundreds	Tens	Ones
2	6	9

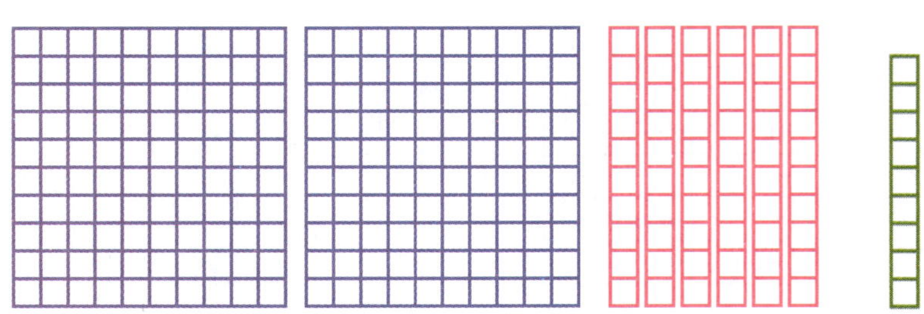

2 hundreds 6 tens 9 ones

Number name = Two hundred sixty-nine

Try This!

Sudha has collected some coins. The number of coins is a 3-digit number.
The number can be represented using blocks as given below. Find the number.

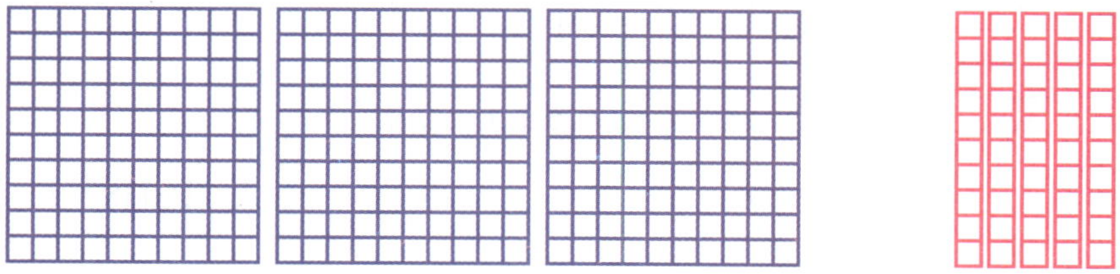

_____ hundreds _____ tens _____ ones

Reading 3-digit Numbers

Let us see how the number 467 is read.

467 is read as four hundred sixty-seven.

H	T	O
4	6	7
↙	↓	↘
Four hundred	sixty	seven

Similarly, the number 658 is read as six hundred fifty-eight.

H	T	O
6	5	8
↙	↓	↘
Six hundred	fifty	eight

Exercise 1.1

1 Fill in the blanks.

a.

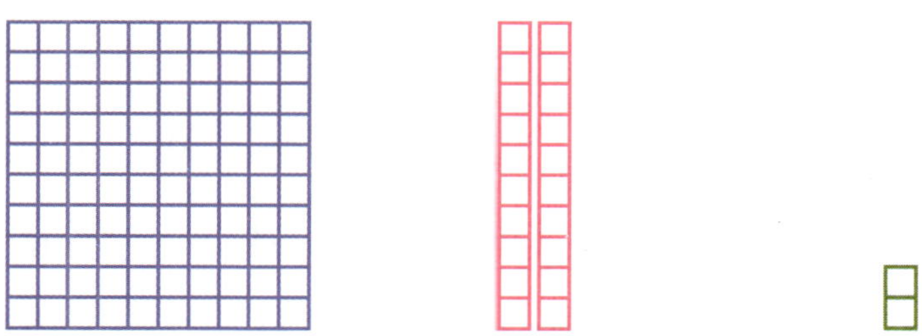

_____ hundreds _____ tens _____ ones

Number name = ______________________________

b.

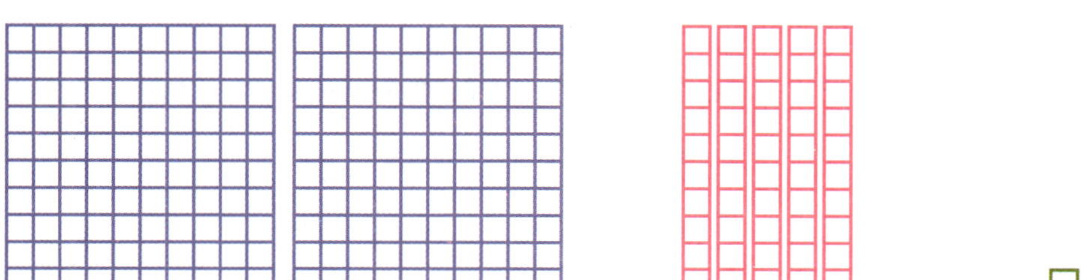

_____ hundreds _____ tens _____ ones

Number name = ______________________________

c. 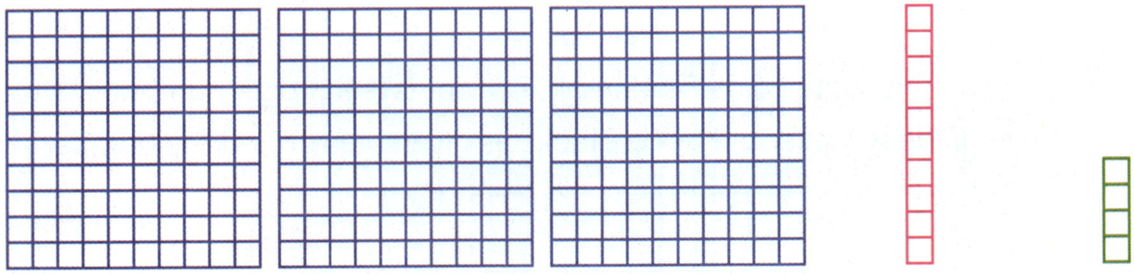

_____ hundreds _____ tens _____ ones

Number name = ____________________

2 Fill in the blanks.

a. 265 = _____ hundreds _____ tens _____ ones

Number name = ____________________

b. 934 = _____ hundreds _____ tens _____ ones

Number name = ____________________

c. 428 = _____ hundreds _____ tens _____ ones

Number name = ____________________

d. 703 = _____ hundreds _____ tens _____ ones

Number name = ____________________

3 Write the numerals for the following number names.

a. Five hundred twenty-eight _______ b. Seven hundred thirteen _______

c. Nine hundred ninety-nine _______ d. Two hundred eighty-seven _______

e. Six hundred thirty-one _______ f. One hundred sixty-four _______

4 Write the four numbers that come after the following numbers.

a. 241, _____, _____, _____, _____ b. 536, _____, _____, _____, _____

c. 912, _____, _____, _____, _____ d. 829, _____, _____, _____, _____

5 Encircle the number that comes after the following numbers.

a. 246		b. 739		c. 549		d. 921	
	312		824		329		922
	247		900		467		578
	189		740		923		216
	200		123		550		190

Representing 3-digit Numbers on the Abacus

532 will be represented on the abacus as:

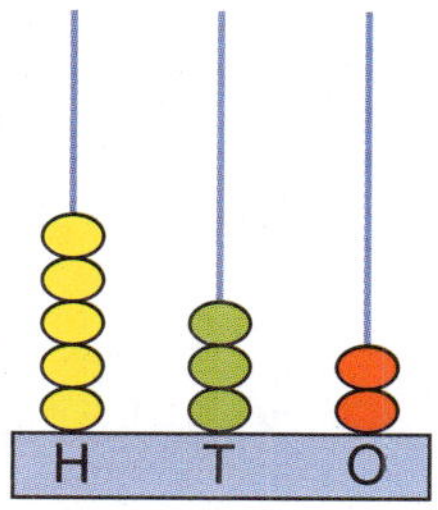

199 will be represented on the abacus as:

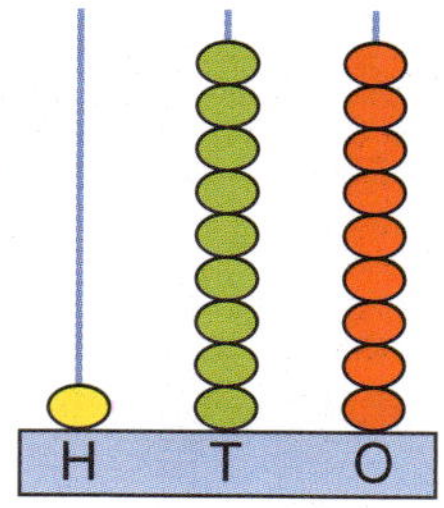

200 will be represented on the abacus as:

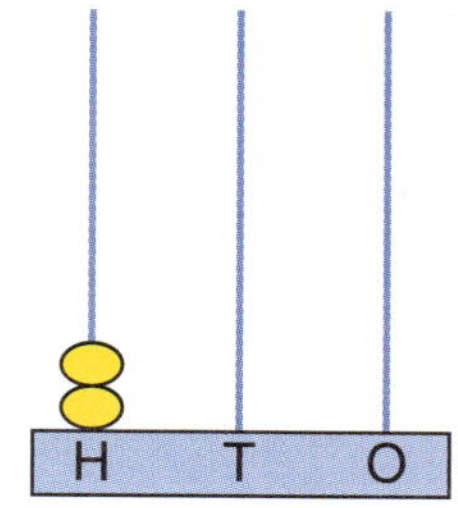

Representing 3-digit Numbers on the Number Line

The number line continues as the numbers get bigger. Some numbers showing parts of the number line are shown below.

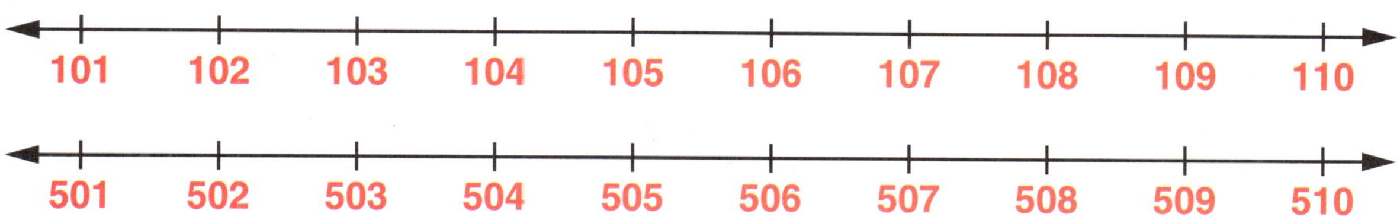

Exercise 1.2

1. **Write the number represented on each abacus.**

a.

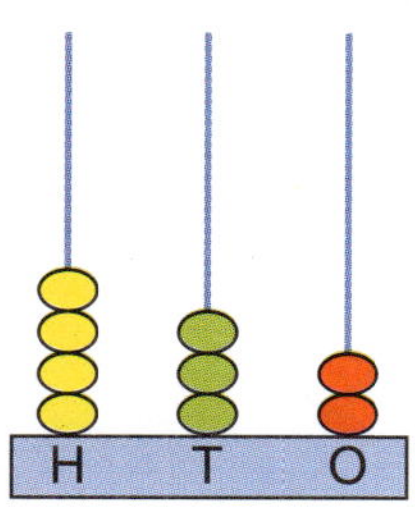

____

b.

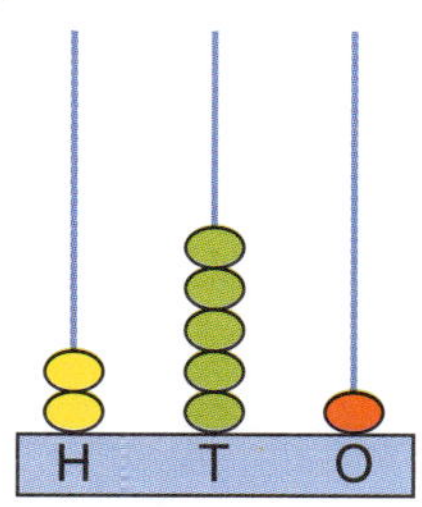

____

c.

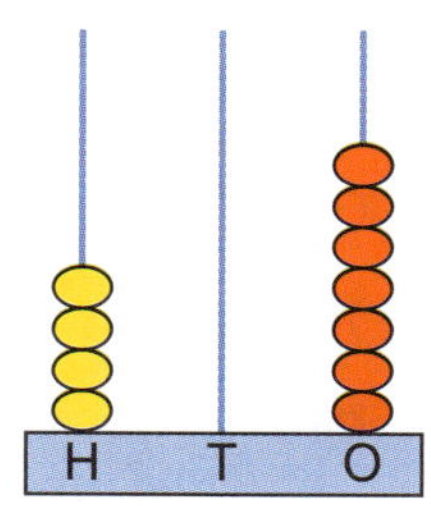

____

d.

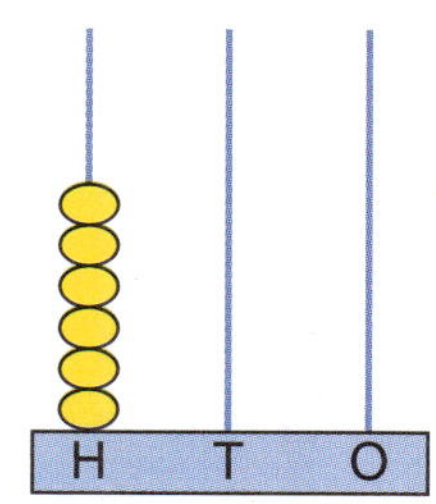

____

2. **Show the following numbers on the given abacuses.**

a. 157

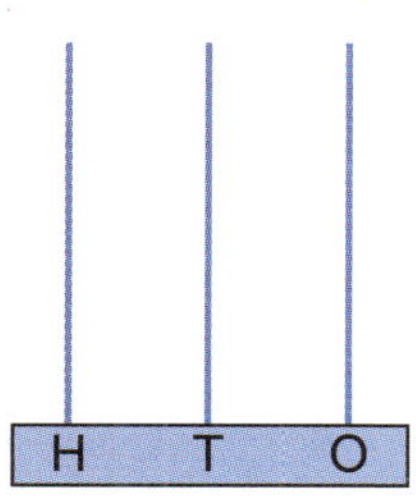

b. 341

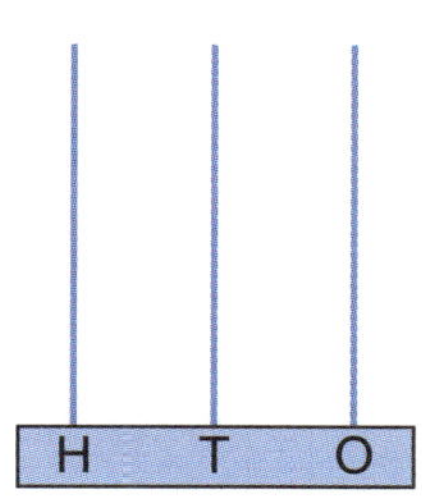

c. 209

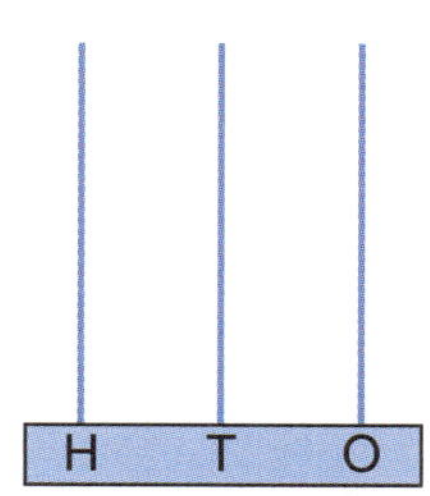

d. 500

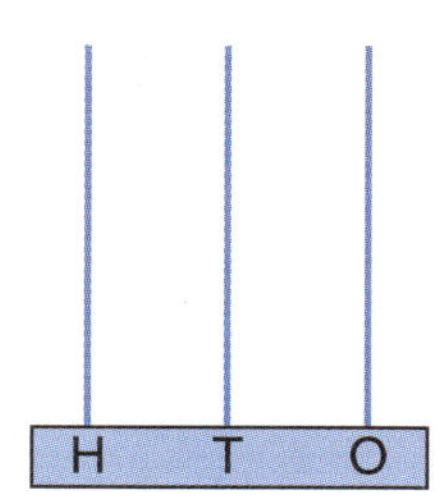

3 **Fill in the missing numbers on the number lines.**

a. 

b. 

c. 

d. 

e. 

Expanded Form of 3-digit Numbers

Let us discuss how to write the expanded form of 3-digit numbers.

Example 1: Write the expanded form of 396.

H T O

3 9 6 = 3 hundreds 9 tens 6 ones

OR

3 9 6 = 300 + 90 + 6

Try This!

1 3 5 = ________ hundred ________ tens ________ ones.

OR

1 3 5 = ________ + ________ + ________.

Example 2: Write the expanded form of 782.

H T O

7 8 2 = 7 hundreds 8 tens 2 ones

OR

7 8 2 = 700 + 80 + 2

Place Value and Face Value

Place Value

Now, let us learn about the place value of 3-digit numbers.

Example 1: In 247:

the place value of **2** is **200**.
the place value of **4** is **40**.
the place value of **7** is **7**.

Example 2: In 569:

the place value of **5** is **500**.
the place value of **6** is **60**.
the place value of **9** is **9**.

Face Value

The face value of a number is the number itself.

Example 3: In 247:

the face value of **2** is **2**.
the face value of **4** is **4**.
the face value of **7** is **7**.

Example 4: In 569:

the face value of **5** is **5**.
the face value of **6** is **6**.
the face value of **9** is **9**.

Exercise 1.3

1 Write the following numbers in expanded form.

H T O

a. 2 7 1 = ______ hundreds ______ tens ______ ones

OR

2 7 1 = ______ + ______ + ______

b. 5 8 3 = ______ hundreds ______ tens ______ ones

OR

5 8 3 = ______ + ______ + ______

c. 4 9 6 = ______ hundreds ______ tens ______ ones

OR

4 9 6 = ______ + ______ + ______

2 Write the place value and the face value of all the digits of the following numbers.

a. 346

Place value of	Face value of
3 = ______	3 = ______
4 = ______	4 = ______
6 = ______	6 = ______

b. 567

Place value of	Face value of
5 = ______	5 = ______
6 = ______	6 = ______
7 = ______	7 = ______

c. 182

Place value of	Face value of
1 = ______	1 = ______
8 = ______	8 = ______
2 = ______	2 = ______

d. 453

Place value of	Face value of
4 = ______	4 = ______
5 = ______	5 = ______
3 = ______	3 = ______

3 **Encircle the place value of the underlined digits of the numbers given below.**

a. 416		b. 573		c. 289		d. 146	
	6		6		9		4
	20		70		50		40
	400		300		20		100

4 **Encircle the face value of the underlined digits of the numbers given below.**

a. 257		b. 378		c. 921		d. 546	
	5		7		20		5
	50		80		1		4
	7		3		9		6

Comparing Numbers

Let us learn to find out the bigger number out of the two given numbers.

Example 1: Fill in the blank with >, < or =.

359 [ ] 721

First we check the digits placed at the hundreds place in both the numbers.

H	T	O		H	T	O
3	5	9		7	2	1

We know that **7** is greater than **3**.

Therefore, 721 [>] 359

Example 2: Fill in the blank with >, < or =.

691 [ ] 628

First we check the digits placed at the hundreds place in both the numbers.

H	T	O		H	T	O
6	9	1		6	2	8

Both the numbers have 6 at the hundreds place.

When the digits at the hundreds place are the same in both the numbers, we check the digits at the tens place in both the numbers.

691   629

9 is bigger than **2**.

Therefore, 691 [>] 629

Example 3: Fill in the blank with >, < or =.

518 ☐ 519

First we check the digits placed at the hundreds place in both the numbers.

H	T	O		H	T	O
5	1	8		5	1	9

Both the numbers have 5 at the hundreds place.

So, now we check the digits placed at the tens place in both the numbers.

Both the numbers have 1 at the tens place. 518 519

So, now we check the digits placed at the ones place in both the numbers. 518 519

9 is bigger than **8**.

Therefore, 518 [<] 519

Example 4: Fill in the blank with >, < or =.

427 ☐ 427

When all the three digits are the same and placed the same way, both the numbers are equal.

Therefore, 427 [=] 427

Exercise 1.4

1 Fill in the blanks with >, < or =.

a. 983 ☐ 421 b. 532 ☐ 189 c. 100 ☐ 700

d. 213 ☐ 213 e. 345 ☐ 369 f. 909 ☐ 909

g. 523 ☐ 549 h. 672 ☐ 678 i. 491 ☐ 423

j. 846 ☐ 850 k. 123 ☐ 129 l. 394 ☐ 392

2 From each set of numbers, encircle the largest number.

a. 539, 416, 278 b. 249, 673, 890

c. 918, 323, 700 d. 654, 752, 851

3 From each set of numbers, encircle the smallest number.

a. 642, 937, 198 b. 349, 582, 731

c. 279, 215, 280 d. 700, 159, 203

Ascending and Descending Order

The meaning of the word 'ascending' is from the smallest to the biggest.

The meaning of the word 'descending' is from the biggest to the smallest.

Ascending Order

Example 1: Arrange the following numbers in ascending order.

596, 243, 987, 126

First we check the digits placed at the hundreds place of all the numbers. The number with the smallest digit in the hundreds place is the smallest number. The next greater digit placed at the hundreds place is the next number and so on.

We can write the order of numbers as shown below.

3	**2**	**4**	**1**
596,	243,	987,	126

These numbers arranged in ascending order are 126, 243, 596, 987.

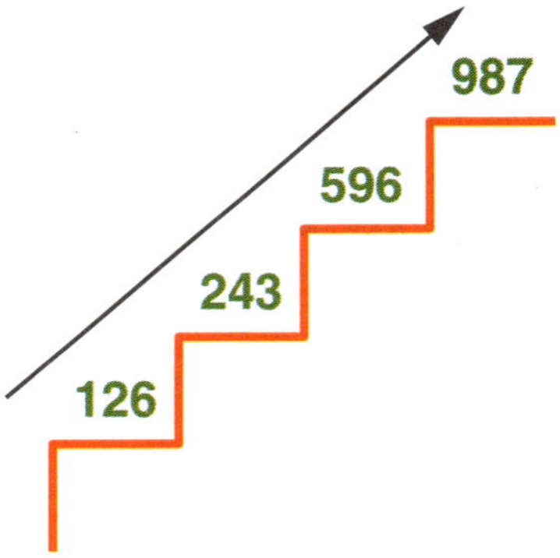

Example 2: Arrange the following numbers in ascending order.

937, 243, 256, 618

First we check the digits placed at the hundreds place.

We see that 243 and 256 both have **2** at the hundreds place. So, we check the digits at the tens place of both these numbers.

H	**T**	**O**
2	4	3

H	**T**	**O**
2	5	6

243 has **4** at the tens place.

256 has **5** at the tens place.

4 is smaller than **5**.

Therefore, **243** is smaller than **256**.

We can write the order of numbers as shown below.

4	**1**	**2**	**3**
937,	243,	256,	618

These numbers arranged in ascending order are
243, 256, 618, 937.

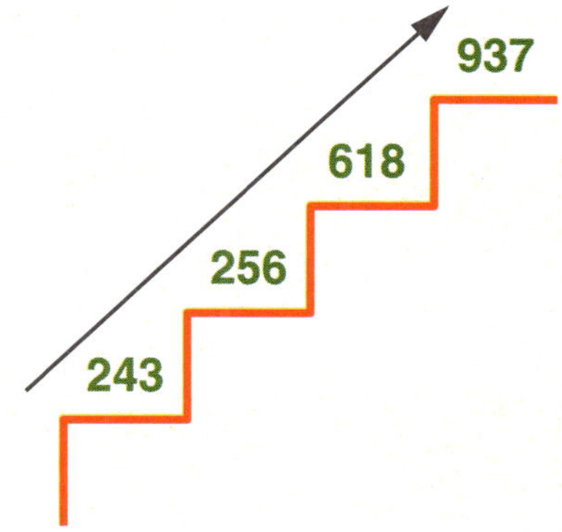

Descending Order

Example 3: Arrange the following numbers in descending order.

349, 910, 734, 825

First we check the digits placed at the hundreds place of all the numbers. The number with the greatest digit placed at the hundreds place is the greatest number. The next smaller digit at the hundreds place is the next number and so on.

We can write the order of numbers as shown below.

4	**1**	**3**	**2**
349,	910,	734,	825

These numbers arranged in descending order are
910, 825, 734, 349.

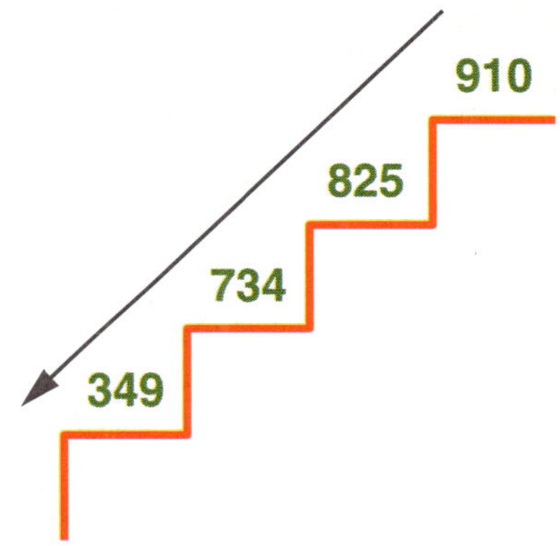

Example 4: Arrange the following numbers in descending order.

376, 512, 804, 590

First we check the digits at the hundreds place of all the numbers. We see that both 512 and 590 have 5 placed at the hundreds place. So, we check the digits placed at the tens place of the numbers.

H	**T**	**O**
5	1	2

H	**T**	**O**
5	9	0

512 has **1** at the tens place.
590 has **9** at the tens place.
Therefore, **590** is bigger than **512**.

We can write the order of numbers as shown below.

4	**3**	**1**	**2**
376,	512,	804,	590

These numbers arranged in descending order are
804, 590, 512, 376.

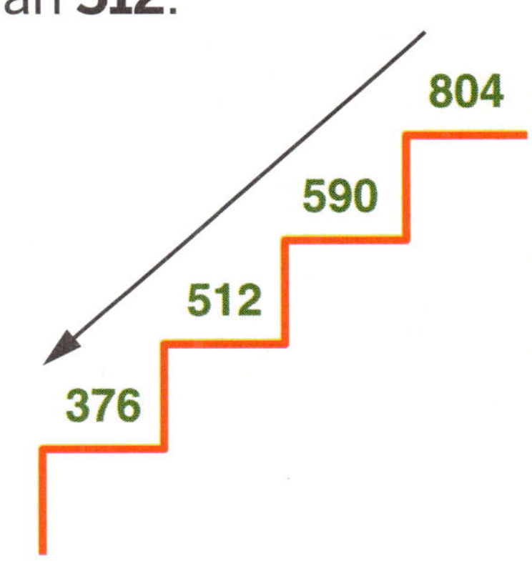

Arranging Numbers in Periods of 10 in Ascending and Descending Order

Examples of Ascending order

a. 210, 220, 230, 240, 250, 260, ...

b. 330, 340, 350, 360, 370, 380, ...

c. 560, 570, 580, 600, 610, ...

d. 880, 890, 900, 910, 920, 930, ...

Examples of Descending order

e. 390, 380, 370, 360, 350, 340, ...

f. 680, 670, 660, 650, 640, 630, ...

g. 730, 720, 710, 700, 690, 680, ...

h. 920, 910, 900, 890, 880, 870, ...

Exercise 1.5

1. **Arrange the following numbers in ascending order.**

   a. 793, 104, 692, 350 ______, ______, ______, ______

   b. 512, 273, 860, 341 ______, ______, ______, ______

   c. 695, 470, 900, 721 ______, ______, ______, ______

   d. 532, 817, 409, 163 ______, ______, ______, ______

2. **Arrange the following numbers in descending order.**

   a. 529, 781, 234, 893 ______, ______, ______, ______

   b. 659, 237, 804, 712 ______, ______, ______, ______

   c. 493, 618, 270, 999 ______, ______, ______, ______

   d. 527, 168, 200, 739 ______, ______, ______, ______

3. **Look at the pattern and complete the numbers (counting by 10) in ascending order.**

   a. 320, 330, ____, ____, ____, ____

   b. 540, 550, ____, ____, ____, ____

   c. 610, 620, ____, ____, ____, ____

   d. 860, 870, ____, ____, ____, ____

   e. 740, 750, ____, ____, ____, ____

   f. 400, 410, ____, ____, ____, ____

4. **Look at the pattern and complete the numbers (counting by 10) in descending order.**

   a. 980, 970, ____, ____, ____, ____

   b. 760, 750, ____, ____, ____, ____

   c. 270, 260, ____, ____, ____, ____

   d. 440, 430, ____, ____, ____, ____

   e. 850, 840, ____, ____, ____, ____

   f. 390,380, ____, ____, ____, ____

Before, After, Between

While learning numbers from 100 to 999, we studied the numbers that come after the given number.

Now, let us practise numbers that come **before** and in **between**.

Example 1: Write the numbers that come before the given numbers.

a. ____, 215 b. ____, 800 c. ____, 901

214, 215 799, 800 900, 901

Example 2: Write the numbers that come in between the given numbers.

a. 235, ____, 237 b. 689, ____, ____, 692

235, 236, 237 689, 690, 691, 692

Exercise 1.6

1. **For each of the following, write the number that comes after the given number.**

   a. 205, ____ b. 724, ____ c. 597, ____

   d. 861, ____ e. 613, ____ f. 286, ____

   g. 939, ____ h. 750, ____ i. 142, ____

2. **For each of the following, write the number that comes before the given number.**

   a. ____, 635 b. ____, 498 c. ____, 923

   d. ____, 717 e. ____, 188 f. ____, 550

   g. ____, 289 h. ____, 830 i. ____, 341

3. **For each of the following, write the number(s) that comes in between the given numbers.**

   a. 167, ____, 169 b. 823, ____, 825

   c. 980, ____, 982 d. 769, ____, 771

   e. 210, ____, ____, 213 f. 543, ____, ____, 546

   g. 629, ____, ____, 632 h. 169, ____, ____, 172.

   i. 399, ____, ____, 402 j. 666, ____, ____, 669

Revision Exercise

1 Fill in the blanks.

a. 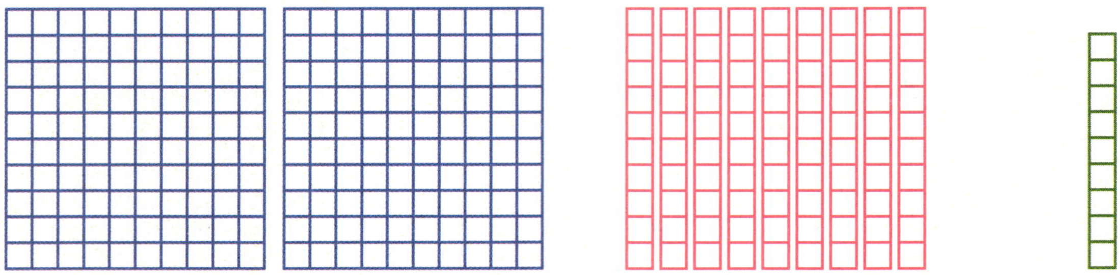

_____ hundreds _____ tens _____ ones

Number name = ____________________

b. 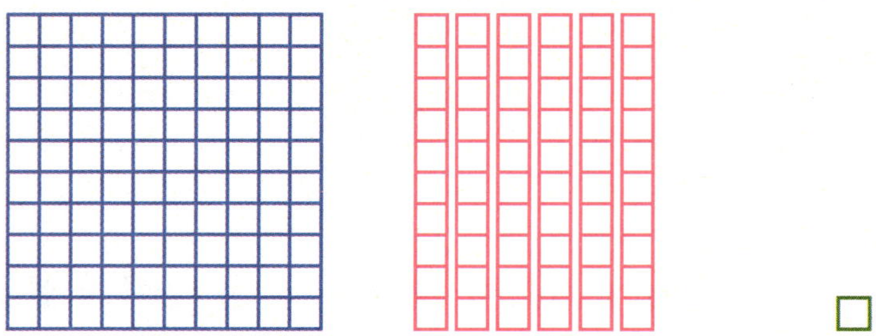

_____ hundreds _____ tens _____ ones

Number name = ____________________

2 Fill in the blanks.

a. 429 = _____ hundreds _____ tens _____ ones

Number name = ____________________

b. 978 = _____ hundreds _____ tens _____ ones

Number name = ____________________

3 Write the numeral for

a. Five hundred six.

b. Nine hundred ninety-nine.

4 Write the four numbers that come after the following numbers.

623, _____, _____, _____, _____

862, _____, _____, _____, _____

5 a. Write the number represented on the abacus.

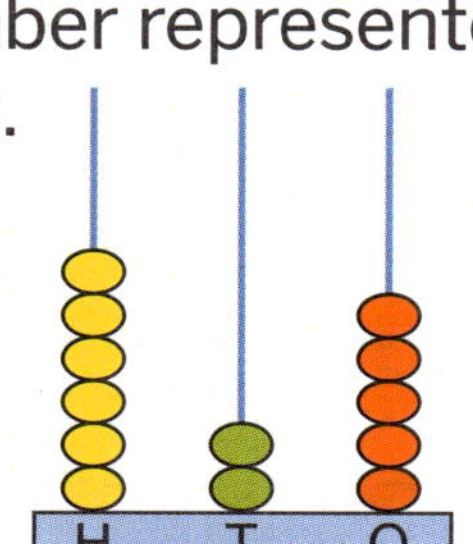

= _____

b. Show 971 on the abacus given below.

6 **Write the missing numbers on the number line given below.**

a. 

b. The expanded form of 935 is

H T O

9 3 5 = _____ hundreds _____ tens _____ ones

OR

9 3 5 = _______ + _______ + _______

c. In 658,

the place value of **6** is _______ .

the face value of **6** is _______ .

7 **Fill in the blanks with >, < or =.**

a. 728 _____ 589

b. 900 _____ 899

c. 625 _____ 673

d. 521 _____ 521

8 **Write the following numbers in ascending order.**

529, 684, 192, 983 _______, _______, _______, _______

9 **Write the following numbers in descending order.**

248, 963, 571, 814 _______, _______, _______, _______

10 **Look at the pattern and fill in the missing numbers.**

a. 430, 440, _______, _______, _______, 480

b. 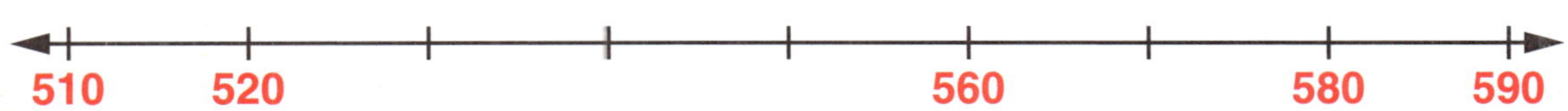

11 **Write the number that comes**

a. before the following number.

_______, 735

b. after the following number.

283, _______

c. in between the following numbers.

948, _______, 950

Worksheet

1 Fill in the blanks.

a. 593 = _____ hundreds _____ tens _____ ones

b. 781 = _____ hundreds _____ tens _____ ones

2 Fill in the blanks.

a. 540 = _____ tens

b. 270 = _____ tens

3 Encircle the largest number and cross out the smallest number in each set of numbers given below.

a. 342, 196, 782

b. 965, 432, 106

c. 318, 235, 648

4 Fill in the blanks with >, < or =.

a. 345 _____ 354

b. 109 _____ 901

c. 544 _____ 545

d. 608 _____ 608

5 Write the number that comes.

a. before the following number
_____, 900

b. after the following number
678, _____

c. in between the following numbers
691, _____,693

For the Curious Mind

From the given numbers, find the correct answers to the questions below and fill in the blanks: 355, 500, 710, 183, 940.

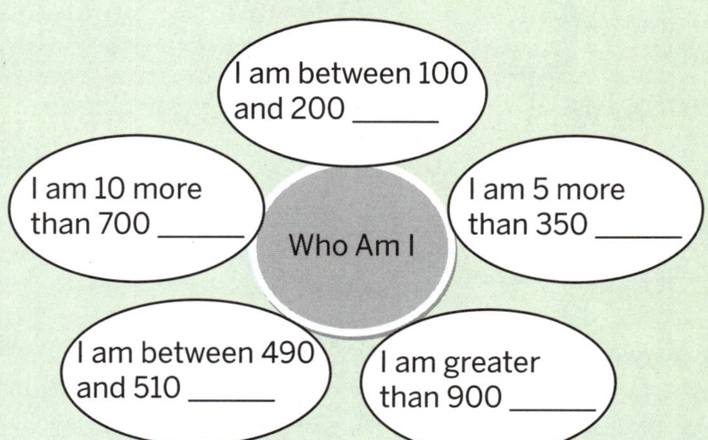

Addition

2

We have learned addition in Class 1. We added 1-digit and 2-digit numbers with and without carrying. Let us revise what we have learned already.

Let's Get Started

1. Fill in the blanks.

   2 + 3 = 5   20 + 30 = 50   200 + 300 = 500

   4 + 5 = ______   40 + 50 = ______   400 + 500 = ______

2. Fill in the blanks.

   5 + 0 = 5   25 + 0 = 25

   479 + 0 = ______   836 + 0 = ______

3. Add the following.

	O
	7
	3
+	8
	___

	T	**O**
	8	5
+	1	2
	___	___

	T	**O**
	3	7
+		8
	___	___

	T	**O**
	5	8
	1	3
+	1	2
	___	___

Cayley's Table

Let's understand the Cayley's Table for addition.

+	1	2	3	4	5
1	2	3	4	5	6
2	3	4	5	6	7
3	4	5	6	7	8
4	5	6	7	8	9
5	6	7	8	9	10

Try These!

Using Cayley's Table, find the following.

3 + 2 = ________

1 + 4 = ________

5 + 2 = ________

3 + 5 = ________

To see the sum of 4 and 5, we go to 4 on the left side column and move to the right till we come under 5. The number given there is 9. This tells us that 4 + 5 = 9.

We can find the sum of any two digits using **Cayley's Table**.

Addition of 3-digit and 2-digit Numbers without Carrying

Let us now learn to add 3-digit and 2-digit numbers.

Example 1: Add 347 and 51.

Step 1

	H	T	O
	3	4	7
+		5	1

First, write these numbers one below the other.

Step 2

	H	T	O
	3	4	7
+		5	1
	3	9	8

We add the ones and the tens columns. The hundreds column has only 3. So, write 3 as the answer in the hundreds place.

Thus, 347 + 51 = 398.

Example 2: Add 825 and 63.

	H	T	O
	8	2	5
+		6	3
	8	8	8

Thus, 825 + 63 = 888.

Exercise 2.1

1 Fill in the blanks.

a. 5 + 0 = ______ b. 46 + 0 = ______

c. 871 + 0 = ______ d. 396 + 0 = ______

2 Fill in the blanks.

a. 2 + 1 = ______
20 + 10 = ______
200 + 100 = ______

b. 5 + 3 = ______
50 + 30 = ______
500 + 300 = ______

c. 7 + 2 = ______
70 + 20 = ______
700 + 200 = ______

d. 4 + 1 = ______
40 + 10 = ______
400 + 100 = ______

3 Add the following.

a.

	H	T	O
	7	3	5
+		6	2

b.

	H	T	O
	9	0	1
+		7	8

c.

	H	T	O
	6	2	7
+		5	1

d.

	H	T	O
	8	4	2
+		3	6

e.

	H	T	O
	4	8	6
+		1	2

f.

	H	T	O
	1	5	3
+		4	4

g.

	H	T	O
	9	2	7
+		6	1

h.

	H	T	O
	5	0	2
+		8	4

i.

	H	T	O
	8	8	3
+		1	5

j.

	H	T	O
	7	0	0
+		2	0

k.

	H	T	O
	3	0	0
+		9	0

l.

	H	T	O
	5	0	0
+		4	0

m.

	H	T	O
	6	1	8
+		7	1

n.

	H	T	O
	5	4	3
+		2	6

o.

	H	T	O
	7	5	7
+		3	2

Addition of Two 3-digit Numbers without Carrying

Now we will learn to add two 3-digit numbers without carrying. Let us understand this through an example.

Example 1: Add 342 and 523.

Step 1

	H	T	O
	3	4	2
+	5	2	3

First, write these numbers one below the other.

Step 2

	H	T	O
	3	4	2
+	5	2	3
			5

Add the numbers in the ones column. 2 + 3 = 5. Write 5 below 3.

Step 3

	H	T	O
	3	4	2
+	5	2	3
		6	5

Next, add the numbers in the tens column. 4 + 2 = 6. Write 6 below 2.

Step 4

	H	T	O
	3	4	2
+	5	2	3
	8	6	5

Then, add the numbers in the hundreds column. 3 + 5 = 8. Write 8 below 5.

Thus, 342 + 523 = 865.

Example 2: Add 123 and 245.

	H	T	O
	1	2	3
+	2	4	5
	3	6	8

Thus, 123 + 245 = 368.

Example 3: Add 578 and 321.

	H	T	O
	5	7	8
+	3	2	1
	8	9	9

Thus, 578 + 321 = 899.

Exercise 2.2

1 **Add the following.**

a.

	H	T	O
	2	3	5
+	6	4	1

b.

	H	T	O
	5	4	1
+	2	3	8

c.

	H	T	O
	3	7	6
+	5	2	1

d.

	H	T	O
	6	4	7
+	3	4	2

e.

	H	T	O
	5	8	9
+	2	1	0

f.

	H	T	O
	4	6	7
+	5	3	2

g.

	H	T	O
	1	6	8
+	7	3	1

h.

	H	T	O
	8	2	3
+	1	4	5

i.

	H	T	O
	7	5	4
+	2	1	2

j.

	H	T	O
	6	3	2
+	1	5	7

k.

	H	T	O
	7	0	3
+	1	9	5

l.

	H	T	O
	5	7	0
+	1	2	8

m.

	H	T	O
	8	5	7
+	1	0	1

n.

	H	T	O
	3	6	2
+	5	0	6

o.

	H	T	O
	5	0	0
+	2	0	0

Addition of Three 2-digit and 3-digit Numbers without Carrying

Addition of three numbers is done in the same way as addition of two numbers. Let us understand through some examples.

Example 1: Add 32, 43 and 11.

	T	O
	3	2
	4	3
+	1	1
	8	6

Thus, 32 + 43 + 11 = 86.

Example 2: Add 213, 504 and 182.

	H	T	O
	2	1	3
	5	0	4
+	1	8	2
	8	9	9

Thus, 213 + 504 + 182 = 899.

Exercise 2.3

1 **Add the following.**

a.

	T	O
	1	2
	4	3
+	3	1

b.

	T	O
	5	4
	3	2
+	1	2

c.

	T	O
	6	8
	1	0
+	1	1

d.

	T	O
	4	0
	1	3
+	2	5

e.

	T	O
	5	2
	3	4
+	1	1

f.

	T	O
	2	7
	5	1
+	2	0

g.

	T	O
	6	2
	1	5
+	1	0

h.

	T	O
	3	5
	2	1
+	1	1

i.

	T	O
	4	3
	2	4
+	1	2

2 **Add the following.**

a.

	H	T	O
	1	2	3
	3	0	4
+	1	5	1

b.

	H	T	O
	6	3	5
	1	4	2
+	2	1	0

c.

	H	T	O
	2	5	7
	3	0	0
+	1	2	1

d.

	H	T	O
	3	4	6
	2	1	2
+	3	1	0

e.

	H	T	O
	5	0	2
	1	7	3
+	1	2	4

f.

	H	T	O
	3	9	6
	1	0	0
+	2	0	0

g.

	H	T	O
	2	0	0
	1	0	0
+	3	0	0

h.

	H	T	O
	5	0	0
	2	0	0
+	1	0	0

i.

	H	T	O
	4	0	0
	3	0	0
+	2	0	0

j.

	H	T	O
	3	4	5
	4	2	1
+	2	1	2

k.

	H	T	O
	6	7	2
	1	0	3
+	1	2	1

l.

	H	T	O
	5	1	4
	1	2	1
+	2	3	0

Addition of Three 2-digit Numbers with Carrying

We have added three 2-digit numbers in Class 1. Let us revise by looking at one example.

Example: Add 23, 15 and 34.

Step 1

	T	O
	2	3
	1	5
+	3	4

First, write these numbers one below the other.

Step 2

	T	O
	1 2	3
	1	5
+	3	4
		2

Add all the digits in the ones column. 3 + 5 + 4 = 12. Write '2' of 12 below 4 and carry forward 1. Place this 1 on top of 2 in the tens column.

Step 3

	T	O
	1 2	3
	1	5
+	3	4
	7	2

Now, add all the digits in the tens column.
1 + 2 + 1 + 3 = 7. Write 7 below 3.

Thus, 23 + 15 + 34 = 72.

Addition of Three 3-digit Numbers with Carrying from Ones to Tens

Let us now learn how to add three 3-digit numbers with carrying from ones to tens by looking at the following example.

Example: Add 356, 123 and 215.

Step 1

	H	T	O
	3	5	6
	1	2	3
+	2	1	5

First, write these numbers one below the other.

Step 2

	H	T	O
	3	$^{1}5$	6
	1	2	3
+	2	1	5
			4

Add all the digits in the ones column. 6 + 3 + 5 = 14. Write '4' of 14 under 5 in the ones column and carry forward 1. Place this 1 above 5 in the tens column.

Step 3

	H	T	O
	3	$^{1}5$	6
	1	2	3
+	2	1	5
		9	4

Now, add all the digits in the tens column. 1 + 5 + 2 + 1 = 9. Place this 9 under 1 in the tens column.

Step 4

	H	T	O
	3	$^{1}5$	6
	1	2	3
+	2	1	5
	6	9	4

Next, add all the digits in the hundreds column. 3 + 1 + 2 = 6. Write 6 under 2 in the hundreds column.

Thus, 356 + 123 + 215 = 694.

Exercise 2.4

1 Add the following.

a.

	H	T	O
	3	1	6
	2	4	3
+	1	2	7

b.

	H	T	O
	4	3	5
	1	0	2
+	2	1	4

c.

	H	T	O
	5	4	6
	1	0	5
+	2	1	3

d.

	H	T	O
	6	2	7
	1	3	5
+	2	0	4

e.

	H	T	O
	7	1	3
	1	2	4
+	1	3	5

f.

	H	T	O
	2	3	9
	5	4	1
+	1	0	6

g.

	H	T	O
	1	4	6
	2	3	2
+	4	1	7

h.

	H	T	O
	5	1	4
	1	3	8
+	2	4	1

i.

	H	T	O
	3	6	8
	2	0	8
+	1	1	2

j.

	H	T	O
	4	5	3
	1	2	6
+		1	5

k.

	H	T	O
	3	2	7
	2	4	3
+		1	6

l.

	H	T	O
	6	2	8
	2	5	4
+		1	2

Addition of Three 3-digit Numbers with Carrying from Ones to Tens to Hundreds

Let us now learn how to add three 3-digit numbers with carrying from ones to tens to hundreds by looking at the following example.

Example 1: Add 346, 175 and 324.

Step 1

	H	T	O
	3	4	6
	1	7	5
+	3	2	4

First, write these numbers one below the other.

Step 2

	H	T	O
	3	$^{1}4$	6
	1	7	5
+	3	2	4
			5

Add all the digits in the ones column. 6 + 5 + 4 = 15. Write '5' of 15 in the ones column and carry forward the '1' of 15. Place this 1 on top of 4 in the tens column.

Step 3

	H	T	O
	$^{1}3$	$^{1}4$	6
	1	7	5
+	3	2	4
		4	5

Now, add all the digits in the tens column. 1 + 4 + 7 + 2 = 14. Write '4' of 14 in the tens column below 2 and carry forward the '1' of 14 on top of 3 in the hundreds column.

Step 4

	H	T	O
	$^{1}3$	$^{1}4$	6
	1	7	5
+	3	2	4
	8	4	5

Now, add all the digits in the hundreds column. 1 + 3 + 1 + 3 = 8. Write 8 in the hundreds column under 3.

Thus, 346 + 175 + 324 = 845.

Example 2:

	H	T	O
	[1]2	[1]4	6
	1	5	3
+	3	7	5
	7	7	4

Example 3:

	H	T	O
	[1]4	[1]5	8
	2	6	3
+	1	5	8
	8	7	9

Exercise 2.5

1. **Add the following.**

a.

	H	T	O
	3	4	5
	2	7	6
+	1	2	3

b.

	H	T	O
	2	6	4
	4	1	7
+	2	8	5

c.

	H	T	O
	1	8	7
	5	0	6
+	2	4	0

d.

	H	T	O
	3	8	9
	4	1	2
+	1	5	3

e.

	H	T	O
	5	3	8
	1	7	4
+	2	4	5

f.

	H	T	O
	4	6	7
	2	3	1
+	1	5	3

g.

	H	T	O
	7	8	4
	1	2	6
+		5	3

h.

	H	T	O
	3	7	5
	4	1	6
+		3	2

i.

	H	T	O
	2	6	8
	5	1	2
+		3	7

j.

	H	T	O
	4	7	6
	1	2	3
+	2	5	4

k.

	H	T	O
	3	6	7
	2	4	3
+	1	8	7

l.

	H	T	O
	5	4	6
	2	7	5
+	1	3	2

m.

	H	T	O
	4	7	3
	2	3	2
+	1	5	1

n.

	H	T	O
	2	6	4
	3	5	0
+	1	3	5

o.

	H	T	O
	1	7	2
	3	5	4
+	2	3	1

Problems on Addition

We add when a quantity increases by the amount given or when we have to find the sum or total. Let us look at the following examples.

Example 1: A bookshop has 343 English books and 536 Mathematics books. What is the total number of English and Mathematics books in the shop?

		H	T	O
English books	=	3	4	3
Mathematics books	=	+ 5	3	6
		8	7	9

Thus, there are 879 English and Mathematics books in the shop.

Hints and Tips

Look out for addition words in any problems. They can give a clue for how to solve the problem.
Addition Words:
Add, total, altogether, sum, plus, more than, increase

Example 2: Amit has 256 red marbles and 135 blue marbles. What is the total number of marbles that Amit has?

		H	T	O
Red marbles	=	2	$^{1}5$	6
Blue marbles	=	+ 1	3	5
		3	9	1

Thus, Amit has 391 marbles in total.

Example 3: In a town there are 357 red cars and 164 blue cars. How many red and blue cars are there in the town?

		H	T	O
Red cars	=	$^{1}3$	$^{1}5$	7
Blue cars	=	+ 1	6	4
		5	2	1

Thus, there are 521 red and blue cars in the town.

Example 4: An ice-cream vendor sold 165 ice creams on Friday, 287 ice creams on Saturday and 345 ice creams on Sunday. How many ice creams did he sell on these 3 days?

		H	T	O
Friday	=	$^{1}1$	$^{1}6$	5
Saturday	=	2	8	7
Sunday	=	+ 3	4	5
		7	9	7

Thus, the vendor sold 797 ice creams in 3 days.

Exercise 2.6

1. 163 people went to a movie hall on Saturday and 425 people went to the movie hall on Sunday. How many people went to the movie hall on Saturday and Sunday?

			H	T	O
Saturday	=				
Sunday	=	+			

Thus, ______ people wen to the movie hall on Saturday and Sunday.

2. Priyanka has ₹ 578. Her mother gives her ₹ 152 more. How much money does Priyanka have now?

			H	T	O
Money she had	=				
Money her mother gave	=	+			

Thus, Priyanka has ______ now.

3. 75 children went to see the circus on Monday, 52 children went to see the circus on Tuesday, 30 children went to see the circus on Wednesday. How many children saw the circus on these three days?

			T	O
Monday	=			
Tuesday	=			
Wednesday	=	+		

Thus, ______ children saw the circle on these three days.

4. In a town, there are 246 red cars, 124 blue cars and 55 yellow cars. What is the total number of cars in the town?

			H	T	O
Red cars	=				
Blue cars	=				
Yellow cars	=	+			

Thus, there are ______ cars in the town.

5. An ice-cream vendor sold 276 ice creams on Friday, 235 ice creams on Saturday and 324 ice creams on Sunday. What is the total number of ice creams he sold on these 3 days?

			H	T	O
Friday	=				
Saturday	=				
Sunday	=	+			

Thus, he sold ______ ice creams on these three days.

6. 629 children come to the school in a school bus. 258 children come by car. What is the total number of children who come to the school by school bus and car?

			H	T	O
School bus	=				
Car	=	+			

Thus, ______ children come to the school by school bus and car.

7. 325 children went for a picnic on Monday and 243 children went on Tuesday. How many children went for the picnic on these two days?

			H	T	O
Monday	=				
Tuesday	=	+			

Thus, ______ children went for the picnic on these two days.

8. In a school, the number of students in Class 1 are 160, in Class 2 are 150 and in Class 3 are 140. What are the total numbers of students in these three classes?

			H	T	O
Class 1	=				
Class 2	=				
Class 3	=	+			

Thus, there are ______ students in the three classes.

Revision Exercise

1 Fill in the blanks.

a. 3 + 1 = ________

30 + 10 = ________

300 + 100 = ________

b. 5 + 2 = ________

50 + 20 = ________

500 + 200 = ________

2 Add the following.

a.

	H	T	O
	7	4	3
+	1	2	5

b.

	H	T	O
	5	8	7
+		1	2

c.

	H	T	O
	6	0	0
+	2	0	0

d.

	T	O
	4	5
	3	1
+	1	2

e.

	T	O
	1	6
	2	4
+	5	3

f.

	H	T	O
	2	3	5
	5	4	2
+	1	2	1

g.

	H	T	O
	1	0	0
	2	0	0
+	3	0	0

h.

	H	T	O
	1	2	3
	3	0	7
+	4	4	1

i.

	H	T	O
	4	3	6
	2	7	5
+	2	1	2

j.

	H	T	O
	1	6	8
	5	3	2
+	1	5	4

k.

	H	T	O
	2	0	4
	1	0	6
+	5	7	0

l.

	H	T	O
	4	4	4
	2	2	2
+	1	1	1

3 The teacher bought 235 milk chocolates and 245 dark chocolates to distribute among the students. What is the total number of chocolates the teacher bought?

		H	T	O
Milk chocolates	=			
Dark chocolates	= +			

Thus, the teacher bought ______ chocolates in total.

4. In a school there are 457 boys and 463 girls. What is the total number of students in the school?

H T O

Boys =

Girls = +

Thus, there are ______ students in total.

5. A bookshop sold 256 English books, 228 Mathematics books and 126 History books in one month. How many books did the bookshop sell in that month?

H T O

English books =

Mathematics books =

History books = +

Thus, the bookshop sold ______ books in that month.

Mental Maths

Your mother sent you to the nearby shop to buy bread and milk. The bread costs ₹22 ad the milk costs ₹28. How much should you pay the shopkeeper for these two items?

____

____

Worksheet

1. **Complete these addition grids.**

a.

+	80	60	90	70
253	333			
185				
693				

b.

+	245	338	152	227
135	380			
226				
641				

2. **Look at the following numbers and answer the questions.**

200 400 100 500

a. Add the smallest and the largest of the given numbers.

b. Which two numbers have the total as 900?

c. Which two numbers have the total as 600?

3. **A cake is made with 350 g flour, 175 g butter and 140 g sugar. What is the total weight of the cake?**

The total weight of the cake is ________ g.

For the Curious Mind

A train travels 435 km from Delhi to Jammu. What is the distance travelled from Delhi to Jammu and back to Delhi?

________ km

Subtraction

3

Subtraction is taking away to find out how much is left. Let us revise what we studied in Class 1.

Let's Get Started

1. Subtract the following:

   a. 5 – 3 = ______ b. 50 – 30 = ______

2. Circle the correct answers.

   a. 40 – 10 =

   10 20 30 40

   b. 70 – 20 =

   30 30 50 60

3. Subtract the following.

a.

	T	O
	8	5
–	6	2

	T	O
	7	9
–		8

b.

	T	O
	5	9
–		8

	T	O
	6	4
–	3	1

c.

	T	O
	2	5
–		6

	T	O
	4	2
–	1	7

d.

	T	O
	2	6
–		7

	T	O
	9	5
–	3	8

e.

	T	O
	3	7
–		9

	T	O
	8	8
–	4	9

Remember

6 – 3 = 3	7 – 1 = 6
60 – 30 = 30	70 – 10 = 60

Remember

When you subtract 0 from a number, its value does not change.

7 – 0 = 7   43 – 0 = 43

69 – 0 = 69   92 – 0 = 92

Subtraction of 1-digit Numbers from 3-digit Numbers without Borrowing

Example: Subtract: 439 – 2

Step 1

	H	T	O
	4	3	9
–			2

First, write the smaller number below the bigger number.

Step 2

	H	T	O
	4	3	9
–			2
			7

Subtract 2 from 9 in the ones column.
That is, 9 – 2 = 7.

Write 7 under 2 in the ones column as the answer.

Step 3

	H	T	O
	4	3	9
–			2
	4	3	7

Since there are no numbers to be subtracted from 3 and 4 under the tens and the hundreds columns, we write 3 in the tens column and 4 in the hundreds column as the answer.

Thus, 439 – 2 = 437.

Subtraction of 2-digit Numbers from 3-digit Numbers without Borrowing

Example 1: Subtract: 564 – 23

Step 1

	H	T	O
	5	6	4
–		2	3

First, write the smaller number below the bigger number.

Step 2

	H	T	O
	5	6	4
–		2	3
			1

Subtract 3 from 4 in the ones column. That is, 4 – 3 = 1.

Write 1 under 3 in the ones column as the answer.

Step 3

	H	T	O
	5	6	4
–		2	3
		4	1

Subtract 2 from 6 in the tens column. That is, 6 – 2 = 4.

Write 4 under 2 in the tens column as the answer.

Step 4

	H	T	O
	5	6	4
–		2	3
	5	4	1

Since there is no number to be subtracted from 5 in the hundreds column, write 5 in the hundreds column as the answer.

Thus, 564 – 23 = 541.

Example 2: Subtract: 785 – 264

	H	T	O
	7	8	5
–	2	6	4
	5	2	1

Thus, 785 – 264 = 521.

Exercise 3.1

1 Write the answers for the following.

a. 9 – 0 = _____ b. 53 – 0 = _____

c. 384 – 0 = _____ d. 721 – 0 = _____

2 Subtract the following.

a.

	H	T	O
	6	9	7
–		8	5

b.

	H	T	O
	8	5	4
–		1	3

c.

	H	T	O
	2	6	5
–		1	3

d.

	H	T	O
	5	7	9
–			4

e.

	H	T	O
	3	7	4
–		5	1

f.

	H	T	O
	3	5	7
–		2	6

g.

	H	T	O
	1	7	2
–		5	0

h.

	H	T	O
	3	4	8
–			5

i.

	H	T	O
	5	6	8
–		2	7

j.

	H	T	O
	4	9	8
–		7	6

k.

	H	T	O
	3	4	1
–		2	0

l.

	H	T	O
	6	7	2
–			1

m.

	H	T	O
	2	4	9
–		1	8

n.

	H	T	O
	2	6	5
–		3	4

o.

	H	T	O
	9	7	3
–		5	0

p.

	H	T	O
	8	1	5
–			2

Subtraction of 3-digit Numbers from 3-digit Numbers without Borrowing

Let us learn to subtract a 3-digit number from a 3-digit number without borrowing with the help of an example.

Example 1: Subtract: 765 – 124

Step 1

	H	T	O
	7	6	5
–	1	2	4

First, write the smaller number below the bigger number.

Step 2

	H	T	O
	7	6	5
–	1	2	4
			1

Subtract 4 from 5 in the ones column. That is, 5 – 4 = 1.

Write 1 under 4 in the ones column as the answer.

Step 3

	H	T	O
	7	6	5
–	1	2	4
		4	1

Subtract 2 from 6 in the tens column. That is, 6 – 2 = 4.

Write 4 under 2 in the tens column as the answer.

Step 4

	H	T	O
	7	6	5
–	1	2	4
	6	4	1

Subtract 1 from 7 in the hundreds column. That is, 7 – 1 = 6.

Write 6 under 1 in the hundreds column as the answer.

Thus, 765 – 124 = 641.

Example 2: Subtract: 875 – 123

	H	T	O
	8	7	5
–	1	2	3
	7	5	2

Thus, 875 – 123 = 752.

Example 3: Subtract: 964 – 521

	H	T	O
	9	6	4
–	5	2	1
	4	4	3

Thus, 964 – 521 = 443.

Exercise 3.2

1 Subtract the following.

a.

	H	T	O
	5	4	3
–	2	1	2

b.

	H	T	O
	5	7	3
–	1	0	2

c.

	H	T	O
	9	8	6
–	2	1	4

d.

	H	T	O
	3	0	0
–	2	0	0

e.

	H	T	O
	6	7	9
−	1	3	8

f.

	H	T	O
	6	8	4
−	5	2	1

g.

	H	T	O
	5	3	7
−	2	1	6

h.

	H	T	O
	6	0	0
−	4	0	0

i.

	H	T	O
	4	8	2
−	3	5	1

j.

	H	T	O
	3	5	7
−	2	1	4

k.

	H	T	O
	4	2	9
−	1	0	8

l.

	H	T	O
	5	0	0
−	1	0	0

m.

	H	T	O
	3	7	6
−	1	2	5

n.

	H	T	O
	4	8	9
−	1	6	7

o.

	H	T	O
	5	4	2
−	3	0	1

p.

	H	T	O
	6	6	6
−	4	4	4

Subtraction of 1-digit Numbers from 3-digit Numbers with Borrowing

Example: Subtract: 972 – 5

Step 1

	H	T	O
	9	7	2
−			5

First, write the smaller number below the bigger number.

Step 2

	H	T	O
	9	6 ~~7~~	12 ~~2~~
−			5

First, subtract 5 from 2. Since 5 is bigger than 2, borrow 1 from 7 in the tens column. The '7' in the tens column becomes '6' and the '2' in the ones column becomes '12'. In the ones column, 12 – 5 = 7.

Step 3

	H	T	O
	9	6 ~~7~~	12 ~~2~~
−			5
	9	6	7

Since there are no numbers to be subtracted from 6 and 9 in the tens and the hundreds columns, write 6 in the tens column and 9 in the hundreds column as the answer.

Thus, 972 – 5 = 967.

Subtraction of 2-digit Numbers from 3-digit Numbers with Borrowing

Example 1: Subtract: 542 – 16

Step 1

	H	T	O
	5	$^{3}\not{4}$	$^{12}\not{2}$
–		1	6

First, write the smaller number below the bigger number.

Step 2

	H	T	O
	5	$^{3}\not{4}$	$^{12}\not{2}$
–		1	6

First, subtract 6 from 2 in the ones column. But since 6 is bigger than 2, borrow 1 from 4 in the tens column. The '4' in the tens column becomes '3' and the '2' in the ones column becomes '12'.

Step 3

	H	T	O
	5	$^{3}\not{4}$	$^{12}\not{2}$
–		1	6
	5	2	6

In the ones column, 12 – 6 = 6.

In the tens column, 3 – 1 = 2.

In the hundreds column, since there is nothing under 5, write 5 as the answer.

Thus, 542 – 16 = 526.

Example 2: Subtract: 635 – 76

Step 1

	H	T	O
	6	3	5
–		7	6

First, write the smaller number below the bigger number.

Step 2

	H	T	O
	6	$^{2}\not{3}$	$^{15}\not{5}$
–		7	6

First, subtract 6 from 5 in the ones column. Since 6 is bigger than 5, borrow 1 from 3 in the tens column. The '3' in the tens column becomes '2' and the '5' in the ones column becomes '15'.

Step 3

	H	T	O
	$^{5}\not{6}$	^{12} $^{\not{2}}\not{3}$	$^{15}\not{5}$
–		7	6
			9

In the ones column, 15 – 6 = 9.

In the tens column, subtract 7 from 2. But since 7 is bigger than 2, borrow 1 from 6 in the hundreds column.

The '2' in the tens column becomes '12' and the '6' in the hundreds column becomes '5'.

Step 4

	H	T	O
	$^{5}\not{6}$	^{12} $^{\not{2}}\not{3}$	$^{15}\not{5}$
–		7	6
	5	5	9

In the tens column, 12 – 7 = 5.

In the hundreds column since there is nothing under 5, write 5 as the answer.

Thus, 635 – 76 = 559.

More examples:

	H	T	O
	3	6 ~~7~~	15 ~~5~~
−		4	6
	3	2	9

	H	T	O
	2	7 ~~8~~	17 ~~7~~
−		3	9
	2	4	8

	H	T	O
	4 ~~5~~	15 ~~5~~ ~~6~~	13 ~~3~~
−		8	5
	4	7	8

	H	T	O
	2 ~~3~~	13 ~~3~~ ~~4~~	12 ~~2~~
−		5	6
	2	8	6

Exercise 3.3

1 Subtract the following.

a.

	H	T	O
	7	3	6
−			9

b.

	H	T	O
	9	2	1
−			4

c.

	H	T	O
	8	6	4
−			5

d.

	H	T	O
	3	7	5
−			6

e.

	H	T	O
	6	6	4
−		3	7

f.

	H	T	O
	3	5	6
−		9	7

g.

	H	T	O
	5	9	2
−		4	8

h.

	H	T	O
	2	4	5
−		8	6

i.

	H	T	O
	3	4	2
−		7	8

j.

	H	T	O
	2	8	3
−		9	5

k.

	H	T	O
	4	5	3
−		1	6

l.

	H	T	O
	4	2	3
−		6	5

m.

	H	T	O
	5	7	4
−		9	6

n.

	H	T	O
	6	2	5
−		2	7

o.

	H	T	O
	8	2	2
−		3	9

p.

	H	T	O
	4	5	1
−		3	3

Subtraction of 3-digit Numbers from 3-digit Numbers with Borrowing

Example 1: Subtract: 935 – 217

Step 1

	H	T	O
	9	3	5
–	2	1	7

First, write the smaller number below the bigger number.

Step 2

	H	T	O
	9	$^{2}\cancel{3}$	$^{15}\cancel{5}$
–	2	1	7

Subtract 7 from 5 in the ones column. 7 is bigger than 5. So, borrow 1 from the '3' in the tens column. The '3' becomes '2' and the '5' in the ones column becomes '15'.

Step 3

	H	T	O
	9	$^{2}\cancel{3}$	$^{15}\cancel{5}$
–	2	1	7
	7	1	8

In the ones column, 15 – 7 = 8. In the tens column, 2 – 1 = 1. In the hundreds column 9 – 2 = 7.

Thus, 935 – 217 = 718.

Example 2: Subtract: 846 – 359

Step 1

	H	T	O
	8	4	6
–	3	5	9

First, write the smaller number below the bigger number.

Step 2

	H	T	O
	8	$^{3}\cancel{4}$	$^{16}\cancel{6}$
–	3	5	9

Subtract 9 from 6. Since 9 is bigger than 6, borrow 1 from 4 in the tens column.

The '4' in the tens place becomes '3' and the '6' in the ones column becomes '16'.

Step 3

	H	T	O
	$^{7}\cancel{8}$	^{13} $^{\cancel{3}}\cancel{4}$	$^{16}\cancel{6}$
–	3	5	9
			7

In the ones column, 16 – 9 = 7. In the tens column, it is not possible to subtract 5 from 3 since 5 is greater than 3. So, borrow 1 from 8 in the hundreds column. The '8' in the hundreds column becomes '7' and the '3' in the tens column becomes '13'.

Step 4

	H	T	O
	$^{7}\cancel{8}$	^{13} $^{\cancel{3}}\cancel{4}$	$^{16}\cancel{6}$
–	3	5	9
	4	8	7

In the tens column, 13 – 5 = 8.

In the hundreds column, 7 – 3 = 4.

Thus, 846 – 359 = 487.

Example 3:

	H	T	O
	6	⁴~~5~~	¹³~~3~~
−	1	2	4
	5	2	9

Example 4:

	H	T	O
	⁶~~7~~	¹³ ~~3~~ ~~4~~	¹²~~2~~
−	3	6	5
	3	7	7

Subtraction with 1 in the Tens Place

Example 5: Subtract: 513 – 246

Step 1

	H	T	O
	5	1	3
−	2	4	6

First, write the smaller number below the bigger number.

Step 2

	H	T	O
	5	⁰~~1~~	¹³~~3~~
−	2	4	6

In the ones column, to subtract 6 from 3, we borrow 1 from the '1' in the tens column. We are left with 0 in the tens column and the '3' in the ones column becomes '13'.

Step 3

	H	T	O
	⁴~~5~~	¹⁰ ~~0~~ ~~1~~	¹³~~3~~
−	2	4	6
			7

In the ones column, 13 – 6 = 7. In the tens column, we cannot subtract 4 from 0. So, we borrow 1 from the '5' in the hundreds column. In the tens place, we get 10 and in the hundreds column we get 4.

Step 4

	H	T	O
	⁴~~5~~	¹⁰ ~~0~~ ~~1~~	¹³~~3~~
−	2	4	6
	2	6	7

In the tens column, 10 – 4 = 6. In the hundreds column, 4 – 2 = 2.

Thus, 513 – 246 = 267.

More examples: (With 1 in the tens column)

	H	T	O
	7	1	2
−	4	3	5

→

	H	T	O
	⁶~~7~~	¹⁰ ~~0~~ ~~1~~	¹²~~2~~
−	4	3	5
	2	7	7

	H	T	O
	8	1	4
−	2	5	7

→

	H	T	O
	⁷~~8~~	¹⁰ ~~0~~ ~~1~~	¹⁴~~4~~
−	2	5	7
	5	5	7

Subtraction with 0 in the Tens Place

Example 6: Subtract: 402 – 136

Step 1

	H	T	O
	(3) ~~4~~	(10) ~~0~~	2
–	1	3	6

To subtract 6 from 2 in the ones column, we will have to borrow from the tens column. But the tens column has '0'. It has nothing to give us. So, we will first borrow 1 from the '4' in the hundreds column. The hundreds column now becomes 3 and the tens column now becomes 10.

Step 2

	H	T	O
	(3) ~~4~~	(9) ~~10~~ ~~0~~	(12) ~~2~~
–	1	3	6

Now, we can borrow 1 from the '10' in the tens column. The ones column now becomes 12 and the tens column becomes 9.

Step 3

	H	T	O
	(3) ~~4~~	(9) ~~10~~ ~~0~~	(12) ~~2~~
–	1	3	6
	2	6	6

In the ones column, 12 – 6 = 6.
In the tens column, 9 – 3 = 6.
In the hundreds column, 3 – 1 = 2.

Thus, 402 – 136 = 266.

More examples: (With 0 in the tens column)

	H	T	O
	9	0	3
–	5	1	6

→

	H	T	O
	(8) ~~9~~	(9) ~~10~~ ~~0~~	(13) ~~3~~
–	5	1	6
	3	8	7

	H	T	O
	7	0	2
–	1	3	5

→

	H	T	O
	(6) ~~7~~	(9) ~~10~~ ~~0~~	(12) ~~2~~
–	1	3	5
	5	6	7

(With 0 in the ones and tens columns)

	H	T	O
	5	0	0
–	2	4	7

→

	H	T	O
	(4) ~~5~~	(9) ~~10~~ ~~0~~	(10) ~~0~~
–	2	4	7
	2	5	3

	H	T	O
	8	0	0
–	3	6	5

→

	H	T	O
	(7) ~~8~~	(9) ~~10~~ ~~0~~	(10) ~~0~~
–	3	6	5
	4	3	5

Exercise 3.4

1 **Subtract the following.**

a.	H	T	O	b.	H	T	O	c.	H	T	O	d.	H	T	O
	6	3	1		7	5	2		4	9	3		2	3	5
−	5	2	4	−	3	4	8	−	1	7	4	−	1	4	7

e.	H	T	O	f.	H	T	O	g.	H	T	O	h.	H	T	O
	5	8	1		6	2	8		5	8	3		7	6	6
−	2	3	9	−	4	0	9	−	1	6	7	−	2	3	8

i.	H	T	O	j.	H	T	O	k.	H	T	O	l.	H	T	O
	3	7	4		7	5	4		8	6	5		5	1	8
−	2	1	6	−	3	2	6	−	2	8	7	−	3	4	9

m.	H	T	O	n.	H	T	O	o.	H	T	O	p.	H	T	O
	9	7	3		9	2	1		9	3	2		3	1	6
−	6	2	5	−	4	5	2	−	7	5	8	−	1	5	7

2 **Subtract the following.**

a.	H	T	O	b.	H	T	O	c.	H	T	O	d.	H	T	O
	8	9	5		5	0	3		7	0	9		5	6	3
−	8	4	9	−	2	7	9	−	4	9	1	−	1	5	6

e.	H	T	O	f.	H	T	O	g.	H	T	O	h.	H	T	O
	3	0	0		6	0	0		9	0	0		7	7	7
−	1	6	8	−	2	7	4	−	3	5	7	−	6	9	9

i.	H	T	O	j.	H	T	O	k.	H	T	O	l.	H	T	O
	4	0	0		8	0	0		5	0	0		5	7	0
−	2	9	1	−	6	3	2	−	3	4	7	−	3	9	9

3 **Subtract the following.**

a.

H	T	O
5	3	2
− 4	1	7

b.

H	T	O
4	9	7
− 1	3	8

c.

H	T	O
7	1	3
− 2	5	4

d.

H	T	O
3	0	8
− 1	2	9

e.

H	T	O
6	2	5
− 1	4	8

f.

H	T	O
9	2	3
− 1	8	5

g.

H	T	O
6	0	5
− 1	3	7

h.

H	T	O
9	1	4
− 6	5	7

i.

H	T	O
7	8	3
− 2	6	9

j.

H	T	O
8	6	2
− 3	9	6

k.

H	T	O
5	0	0
− 1	9	2

l.

H	T	O
2	0	0
− 1	3	5

Word Problems on Subtraction

Hints and Tips

Look out for subtraction words in any problem. They can give a clue to solve the problem.

Subtraction Words:
Subtract, take away, minus, less than, fewer, difference, reduce

We subtract when a quantity reduces by an amount given or when we have to find the difference.

Example 1: Out of 752 children in a school, 341 were boys. How many girls were there?

	H	T	O
Total number of children	7	5	2
Number of boys	− 3	4	1
	4	1	1

Thus, there were 411 girls.

Example 2: Out of 520 people travelling on a train, 165 were children. How many were adults?

	H	T	O
Total number of people	$\overset{4}{\not 5}$	$\overset{11}{\not 1}\!\!\!\not 2$	$\overset{10}{\not 0}$
Number of children	− 1	6	5
	3	5	5

Thus, there were 355 adults.

Example 3: Rajiv had 200 marbles. He lost 25 of them. How many marbles were left with Rajiv?

		H	T	O
			9	
Total number of marbles		1 ~~2~~	~~10~~ 10 0	10 ~~0~~
Marbles he lost	–		2	5
		1	7	5

Thus, 175 marbles were left with Rajiv.

Exercise 3.5

1. A bookshop had 985 books. 110 books got sold in 1 week. How many books were left in the shop?

		H	T	O
Total number of books				
Books sold	–			

Thus, ________ books were left in the shop.

2. The total number of students in a school were 874. On Monday, 12 students were absent. How many were present?

		H	T	O
Total number of students				
Number of students absent	–			

Thus, ________ students were present.

3. 354 children sat for an examination. 328 children passed in the examination. How many children did not pass?

		H	T	O
Total number of children				
Number of children passed	–			

Thus, ________ children did not pass.

4. Anil earned ₹925 in one week. He spent ₹57. How much money was left with him?

		H	T	O
Money earned				
Money spent	–			

Thus, ________ was left with Anil.

5. An ice cream vendor had 215 ice creams. He sold 78 ice creams in one day. How many ice creams were left with him?

	H	T	O
Total number of ice creams			
Number of ice creams sold −			

Thus, ________ ice creams were left with him.

6. A movie hall had 450 seats. 429 seats were occupied. How many seats were not occupied?

	H	T	O
Total number of seats			
Number of seats occupied −			

Thus, ________ seats were not occupied.

7. Reena had 300 marbles. Rajan had 179 marbles. How many more marbles did Reena have than Rajan?

	H	T	O
Number of marbles with Reena			
Number of marbles with Rajan −			

Thus, Reena had ________ more marbles than Rajan.

8. Out of 958 students in a school, 723 like to play cricket. How many do not like to play cricket?

	H	T	O
Total number of students			
Number of students who like to play cricket −			

Thus, ________ students do not like to play cricket.

9 Rahul put up 250 balloons on his birthday. 25 balloons burst. How many balloons were still left?

		H	T	O
Total balloons				
Balloons that burst	−			

Thus, ________ balloons were left.

10 Sheena carried 124 chocolates to school on her birthday. She gave away 113 chocolates to her friends. How many chocolates were left with her?

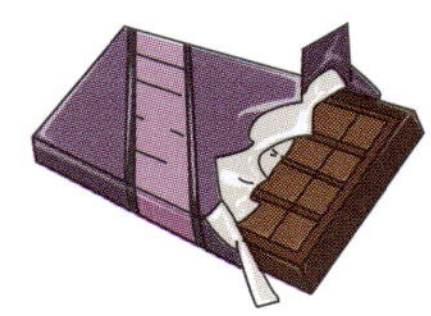

		H	T	O
Total chocolates				
Chocolates she gave away	−			

Thus, ________ chocolates were left with her.

Word Problems Involving Addition and Subtraction

The problems we just did involved only subtraction. Now, we will understand problems that involve addition and subtraction.

Example 1: Rajat had 125 marbles. His mother bought him 150 more marbles. Then he lost 30 marbles. How many marbles does he have now?

Number of marbles Rajat had = 125

Number of marbles bought by his mother = 150

Total marbles = 125 + 150

	H	T	O
	1	2	5
+	1	5	0
	2	7	5

Number of marbles he lost = 30

Marbles left with him = 275 − 30

	H	T	O
	2	7	5
−		3	0
	2	4	5

Thus, he had 245 marbles.

Example 2: There were 256 cars parked in the parking lot. 123 cars drove away. 35 more cars came and parked. How many cars were there in the parking lot now?

Number of cars parked = 256

Number of cars that went = 123

Total cars left = 256 − 123

	H	T	O
	2	5	6
−	1	2	3
	1	3	3

Number of cars that came = 35

Total number of cars = 133 + 35

	H	T	O
	1	3	3
+		3	5
	1	6	8

Thus, total number of cars was 168.

Exercise 3.6

1. There were 352 trees in a forest. 123 more trees were planted. Then, 46 trees were cut. How many trees were left in the forest?

Total number of trees = ______

Number of trees planted = ______

Total number of trees = ______ + ______

	H	T	O
+			

Number of trees cut = ______

Total number of trees left = ______ − ______

	H	T	O
−			

Thus, ______ trees were left in the forest.

2. In a garden, there were 125 flowers. 36 flowers died. 75 flowers grew. Now, how many flowers are there in the garden?

Thus, there were ______ flowers in the garden.

3. Seema had ₹500. Her mother gave her ₹220 more. She spent ₹130 to buy a doll. How much money does Seema have now?

Thus, Seema has ₹ ________.

4. A baker baked 132 cakes in the morning and 120 cakes in the afternoon. In the evening, he sold 250 cakes. How many cakes were left?

Thus, ________ cakes were left.

5. Rajeev had 352 stamps. He gave away 35 stamps to his friends. He managed to collect 121 more stamps. How many stamps does Rajeev have now?

Thus, Rajeev has ________ stamps.

6. There were 102 children in a park. 56 children went back home. 94 more children came to the park. How many children are there in the park now?

Thus, there are ________ children in the park.

7. 342 people came in the morning to watch a cricket match. In the afternoon, 100 people left. In the evening, 256 more people came. How many people were there in the evening?

Thus, there were ________ people in the evening.

Revision Exercise

1 **Solve the following.**

a. 4 – 3 = _____
40 – 30 = _____
400 – 300 = _____

b. 9 – 5 = _____
90 – 50 = _____
900 – 500 = _____

c. 5 – 2 = _____
50 – 20 = _____
500 – 200 = _____

2 **Subtract the following.**

a.

	H	T	O
	8	2	9
–	3	1	7

b.

	H	T	O
	7	3	5
–	2	1	6

c.

	H	T	O
	5	3	2
–		4	9

d.

	H	T	O
	7	2	0
–	4	7	3

e.

	H	T	O
	7	3	6
–		2	5

f.

	H	T	O
	9	4	2
–	3	8	5

g.

	H	T	O
	7	8	3
–			4

h.

	H	T	O
	5	0	2
–		3	8

i.

	H	T	O
	5	4	8
–			6

j.

	H	T	O
	6	7	1
–		3	8

k.

	H	T	O
	6	1	3
–	2	5	4

l.

	H	T	O
	9	0	0
–		4	7

3 357 people bought tickets for a movie show. Only 309 people came to watch it. How many people did not come to watch the movie?

Thus, ________ people did not come to watch the movie.

4 Priyanka had ₹755. She spent ₹297 out of it. Her mother gave her ₹432 more. How much money did Priyanka have now?

Thus, Priyanka had ________.

Worksheet

1 Look at the heights of these sunflowers and answer these questions.

a. How much taller is Sunflower A than Sunflower B? ______ cm

b. How much taller is Sunflower B than Sunflower C? ______ cm

c. If Sunflower D grows to be the same height as Sunflower A, how many more centimetres will it need to grow? ______ cm

d. What is the difference in height between Sunflower D and Sunflower E? ______ cm

e. How much shorter is Sunflower E than Sunflower B? ______ cm

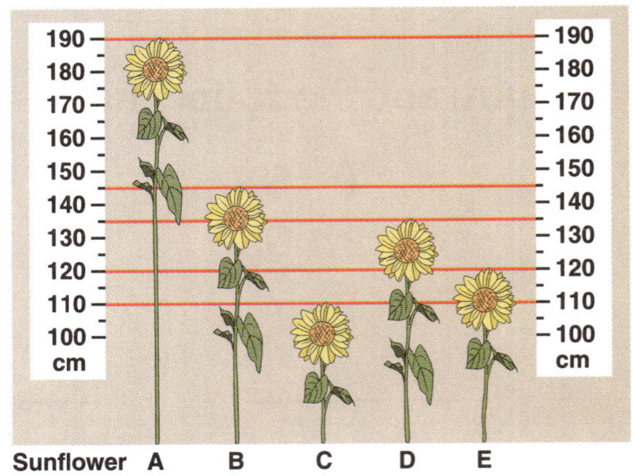

Mental Maths

1. Subtract one hundred from 287. ______________
2. Subtract the greatest 2-digit number from the greatest 3-digit number. ______________
3. From 500, subtract the number that comes after 199. ______________

For the Curious Mind

There are 525 students in School A and 635 students in School B. How many more students are there in School B than in School A?

Multiplication

4

Let's Get Started

We studied multiplication of numbers in Class 1. Let us revise.

Multiply the following.

1. a. $7 \times 2 =$ ______ b. $9 \times 1 =$ ______ c. $0 \times 5 =$ ______

   d. $4 \times 5 =$ ______ e. $5 \times 10 =$ ______ f. $0 \times 13 =$ ______

Multiplication as Repeated Addition

As we learned earlier, multiplication is repeated addition.

When we have to add the same thing a number of times, we can calculate it faster using multiplication.

Consider 3 groups of marbles shown below.

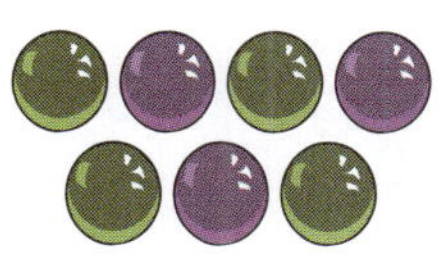 + 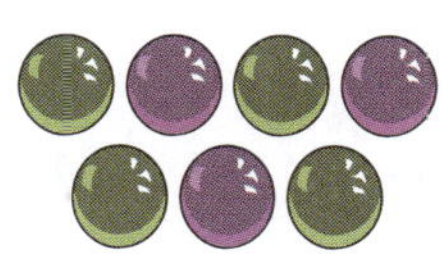 + 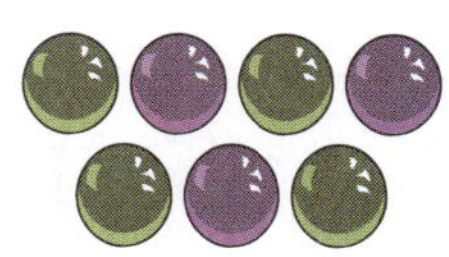 **= 21**

Number of marbles in each group = 7

Number of groups = 3

Therefore, $3 \times 7 = 21$

Also, $7 + 7 + 7 = 3 \times 7 = 21$

Consider 4 groups of trees shown here.

 +  +  +  **= 8**

Number of trees in each group = 2

Number of groups = 4

Therefore, 4 × 2 = 8

Exercise 4.1

1 **Fill in the blanks and write the multiplication statement for the following.**

a.  = 18

Number of spoons in each group = ______

Number of groups = ______

Therefore, ______ × ______ = ______

b.  = 12

Number of children in each group = ______

Number of groups = ______

Therefore, ______ × ______ = ______

2 **Fill in the blanks.**

a. 

= ______ × ______

b. 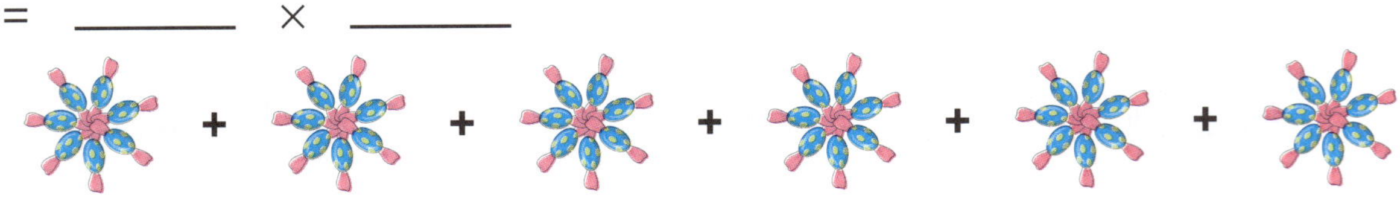

= ______ × ______

c. 

= ______ × ______

3 **Write the multiplication statements for the following repeated additions.**

a. 2 + 2 + 2 + 2 + 2 + 2 + 2 = ______ × ______

b. 6 + 6 + 6 + 6 = ______ × ______

c. 9 + 9 + 9 + 9 + 9 = ______ × ______

d. 10 + 10 + 10 = ______ × ______

4 **Match the pictures in column A with the multiplication facts in column B.**

	A	B
a.		5×3
b.		4×3
c.	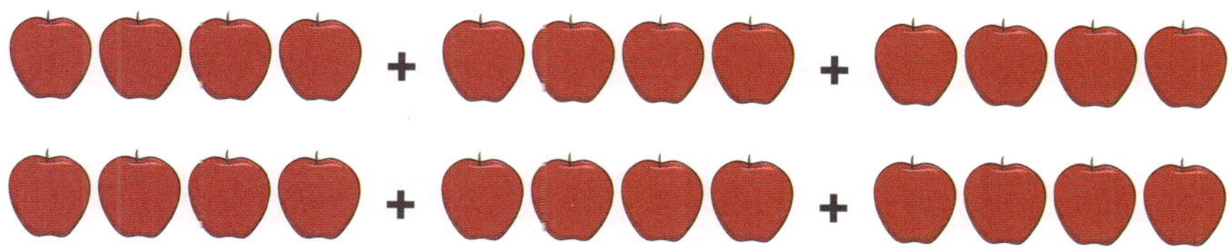	4×2
d.	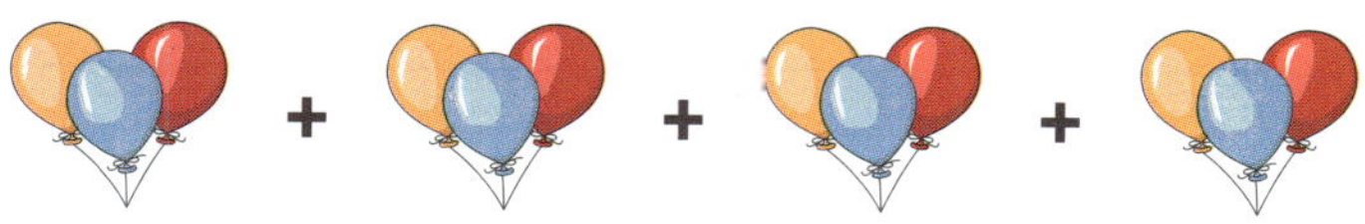	9×2
e.		6×4

Multiplication Facts

1. In a multiplication statement like

$$2 \times 3 = 6$$

Multiplier (2), **Multiplicand** (3), **Product** (6)

2 is the **multiplier**.

3 is the **multiplicand**.

6 is the **product**.

2.  = 6

3×2 = 2×3

We notice that $2 \times 3 = 3 \times 2 = 6$.

In the same way,

$4 \times 5 = 5 \times 4$

$6 \times 2 = 2 \times 6$

Hence, the order of numbers in multiplication does not matter. The product remains the same.

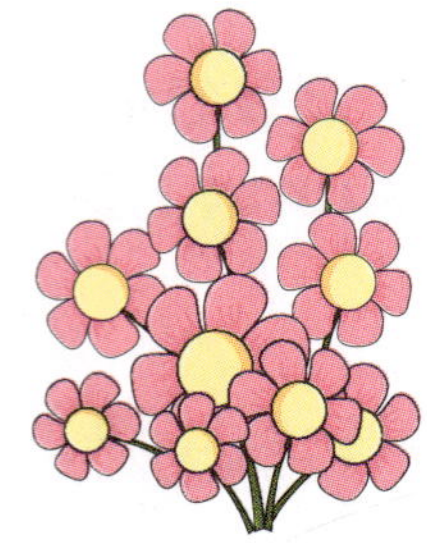

3. If a number is multiplied by 1, the value of the product is the same as the number.

$2 \times 1 = 2$ $\quad$ $3 \times 1 = 3$

4. If a number is multiplied by 0, the value of the product is 0.

$2 \times 0 = 0$ $\quad$ $3 \times 0 = 0$

Exercise 4.2

1 Fill in the blanks.

a. In $3 \times 5 = 15$,
the multiplier is ________.
the multiplicand is ________.
the product is ________.

b. In $4 \times 2 = 8$,
the multiplier is ________.
the multiplicand is ________.
the product is ________.

c. In $10 \times 5 = 50$,
the multiplier is ________,
the multiplicand is ________,
the product is ________.

d. In $25 \times 1 = 25$,
the multiplier is ________,
the multiplicand is ________,
the product is ________.

2 Fill in the blanks.

a. $2 \times 3 =$ ________ $\times 2$

b. $4 \times 6 =$ ________ $\times 4$

c. $3 \times 9 = 9 \times$ ________

d. $55 \times 7 = 7 \times$ ________

3 Fill in the blanks.

a. $3 \times 1 =$ ________

b. $1 \times 5 =$ ________

c. $10 \times 1 =$ ________

d. $7 \times 1 =$ ________

4 Fill in the blanks.

a. $2 \times 0 =$ ________

b. $1 \times 0 =$ ________

c. $3 \times 0 =$ ________

d. $4 \times 0 =$ ________

Multiplication Tables

Table of 1

1	1 × 1 = 1
1 + 1	2 × 1 = 2
1 + 1 + 1	3 × 1 = 3
1 + 1 + 1 + 1	4 × 1 = 4
1 + 1 + 1 + 1 + 1	5 × 1 = 5
1 + 1 + 1 + 1 + 1 + 1	6 × 1 = 6
1 + 1 + 1 + 1 + 1 + 1 + 1	7 × 1 = 7
1 + 1 + 1 + 1 + 1 + 1 + 1 + 1	8 × 1 = 8
1 + 1 + 1 + 1 + 1 + 1 + 1 + 1+ 1	9 × 1 = 9
1 + 1 + 1 + 1 + 1 + 1 + 1 + 1 + 1 + 1	10 × 1 = 10

Try These!

2 × 1 = ____

5 × 1 = ____

7 × 1 = ____

10 × 1 = ____

Note

The product of a number and 1 is the number itself.

On Number Line

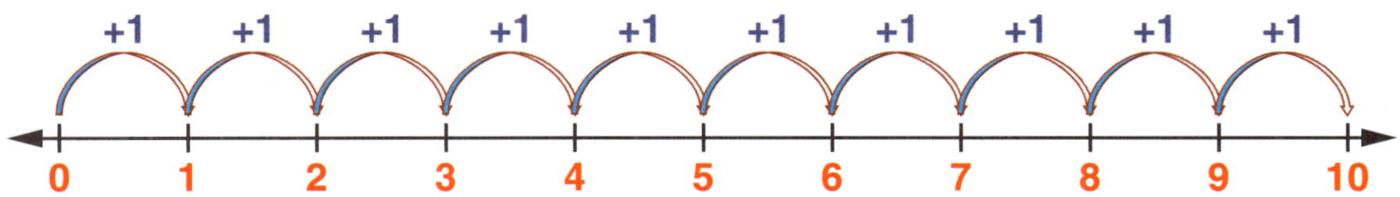

Table of 2

2	1 × 2 = 2
2 + 2	2 × 2 = 4
2 + 2 + 2	3 × 2 = 6
2 + 2 + 2 + 2	4 × 2 = 8
2 + 2 + 2 + 2 + 2	5 × 2 = 10
2 + 2 + 2 + 2 + 2 + 2	6 × 2 = 12
2 + 2 + 2 + 2 + 2 + 2 + 2	7 × 2 = 14
2 + 2 + 2 + 2 + 2 + 2 +2 + 2	8 × 2 = 16
2 + 2 + 2 + 2 + 2 + 2 + 2 + 2 + 2	9 × 2 = 18
2 + 2 + 2 + 2 + 2+ 2 + 2 + 2 + 2 + 2	10 × 2 = 20

Try These!

3 × 2 = ____

5 × 2 = ____

7 × 2 = ____

9 × 2 = ____

Note

The products in the table of 2 end with 0, 2, 4, 6 or 8.

On Number Line

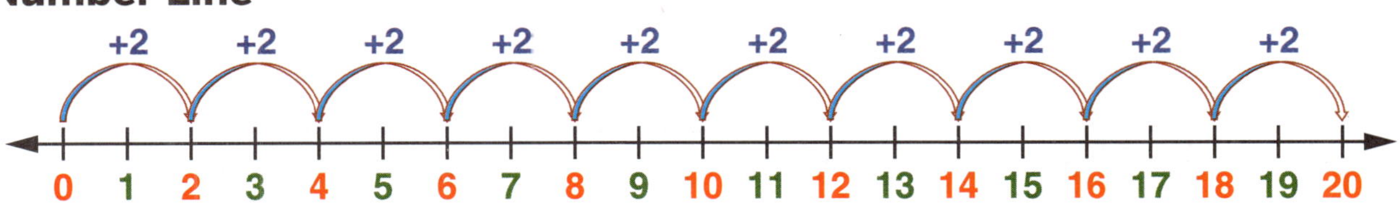

Try These!

1 × 3 = ____

3 × 3 = ____

5 × 3 = ____

8 × 3 = ____

Table of 3

3	1 × 3 = 3
3 + 3	2 × 3 = 6
3 + 3 + 3	3 × 3 = 9
3 + 3 + 3 + 3	4 × 3 = 12
3 + 3 + 3 + 3 + 3	5 × 3 = 15
3 + 3 + 3 + 3 + 3 + 3	6 × 3 = 18
3 + 3 + 3 + 3 + 3 + 3 + 3	7 × 3 = 21
3 + 3 + 3 + 3 + 3 + 3 + 3 + 3	8 × 3 = 24
3 + 3 + 3 + 3 + 3 + 3 + 3 + 3 + 3	9 × 3 = 27
3 + 3 + 3 + 3 + 3 + 3 + 3 + 3 + 3 + 3	10 × 3 = 30

On Number Line

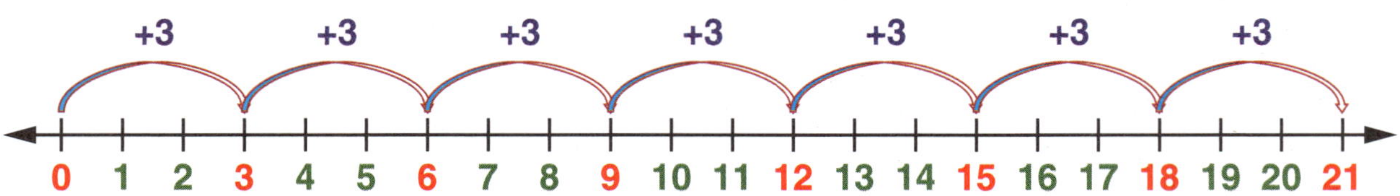

Try These!

1 × 4 = ____

2 × 4 = ____

5 × 4 = ____

7 × 4 = ____

Table of 4

4	1 × 4 = 4
4 + 4	2 × 4 = 8
4 + 4 + 4	3 × 4 = 12
4 + 4 + 4 + 4	4 × 4 = 16
4 + 4 + 4 + 4 + 4	5 × 4 = 20
4 + 4 +4 + 4 + 4 + 4	6 × 4 = 24
4 + 4 + 4 + 4 + 4 + 4 + 4	7 × 4 = 28
4 + 4 + 4 + 4 + 4 + 4 + 4 + 4	8 × 4 = 32
4 + 4 + 4 + 4 + 4 + 4 + 4 + 4 + 4	9 × 4 = 36
4 + 4 + 4 + 4 + 4 + 4 + 4 + 4 + 4 + 4	10 × 4 = 40

On Number Line

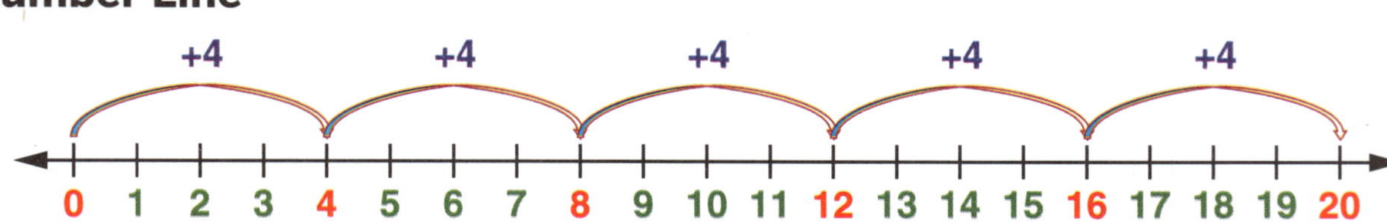

Table of 5

5	1 × 5 = 5
5 + 5	2 × 5 = 10
5 + 5 + 5	3 × 5 = 15
5 + 5 + 5 + 5	4 × 5 = 20
5 + 5 + 5 + 5 + 5	5 × 5 = 25
5 + 5 + 5 + 5 + 5 + 5	6 × 5 = 30
5 + 5 + 5 + 5 + 5 + 5 + 5	7 × 5 = 35
5 + 5 + 5 + 5 + 5 + 5 + 5 + 5	8 × 5 = 40
5 + 5 + 5 + 5 + 5 + 5 + 5 + 5 + 5	9 × 5 = 45
5 + 5 + 5 + 5 + 5 + 5 + 5 + 5 + 5 + 5	10 × 5 = 50

Try These!

1 × 5 = ____

4 × 5 = ____

6 × 5 = ____

9 × 5 = ____

Note

All products in the table of 5 end with 5 and 0 alternatively.

On Number Line

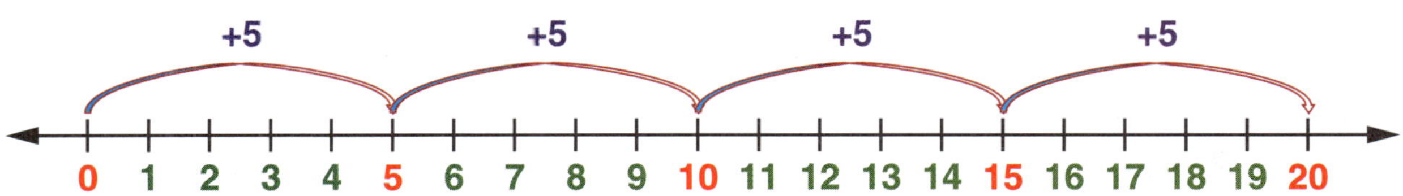

Table of 6

6	1 × 6 = 6
6 + 6	2 × 6 = 12
6 + 6 + 6	3 × 6 = 18
6 + 6 + 6 + 6	4 × 6 = 24
6 + 6 + 6 + 6 + 6	5 × 6 = 30
6 + 6 + 6 + 6 + 6 + 6	6 × 6 = 36
6 + 6 + 6 + 6 + 6 + 6 + 6	7 × 6 = 42
6 + 6 + 6 + 6 + 6 + 6 + 6 + 6	8 × 6 = 48
6 + 6 + 6 + 6 + 6 + 6 + 6 + 6 + 6	9 × 6 = 54
6 + 6 + 6 + 6 + 6 + 6 + 6 + 6 + 6 + 6	10 × 6 = 60

Try These!

1 × 6 = ____

3 × 6 = ____

5 × 6 = ____

10 × 6 = ____

On Number Line

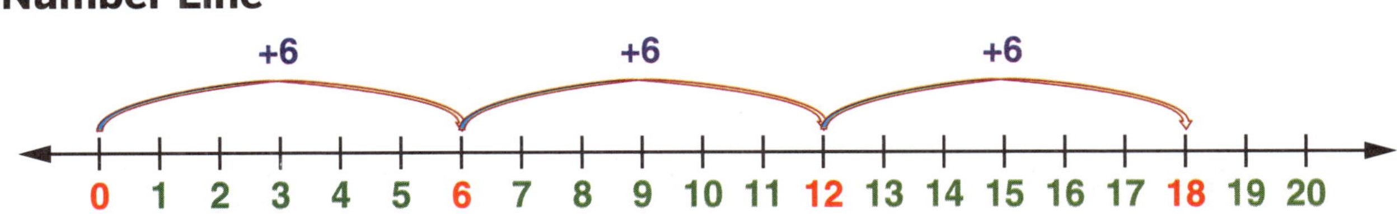

Table of 7

Try These!

1 × 7 = ____

3 × 7 = ____

6 × 7 = ____

9 × 7 = ____

7	1 × 7 = 7
7 + 7	2 × 7 = 14
7 + 7 + 7	3 × 7 = 21
7 + 7 + 7 + 7	4 × 7 = 28
7 + 7 + 7 + 7 + 7	5 × 7 = 35
7 + 7 + 7 + 7 + 7 + 7	6 × 7 = 42
7 + 7 + 7 + 7 + 7 + 7 + 7	7 × 7 = 49
7 + 7 + 7 + 7 + 7 + 7 + 7 + 7	8 × 7 = 56
7 + 7 + 7 + 7 + 7 + 7 + 7 + 7 + 7	9 × 7 = 63
7 + 7 + 7 + 7 + 7 + 7 + 7 + 7 + 7 + 7	10 × 7 = 70

On Number Line

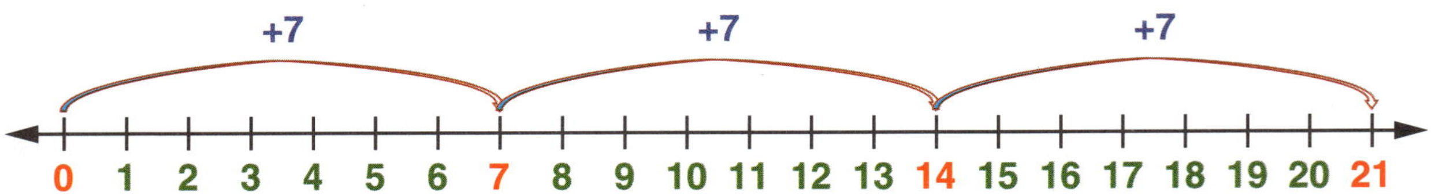

Table of 8

Try These!

2 × 8 = ____

5 × 8 = ____

6 × 8 = ____

9 × 8 = ____

8	1 × 8 = 8
8 + 8	2 × 8 = 16
8 + 8 + 8	3 × 8 = 24
8 + 8 + 8 + 8	4 × 8 = 32
8 + 8 + 8 + 8 + 8	5 × 8 = 40
8 + 8 + 8 + 8 + 8 + 8	6 × 8 = 48
8 + 8 + 8 + 8 + 8 + 8 + 8	7 × 8 = 56
8 + 8 + 8 + 8 + 8 + 8 + 8 + 8	8 × 8 = 64
8 + 8 + 8 + 8 + 8 + 8 + 8 + 8 + 8	9 × 8 = 72
8 + 8 + 8 + 8 + 8 + 8 + 8 + 8 + 8 + 8	10 × 8 = 80

On Number Line

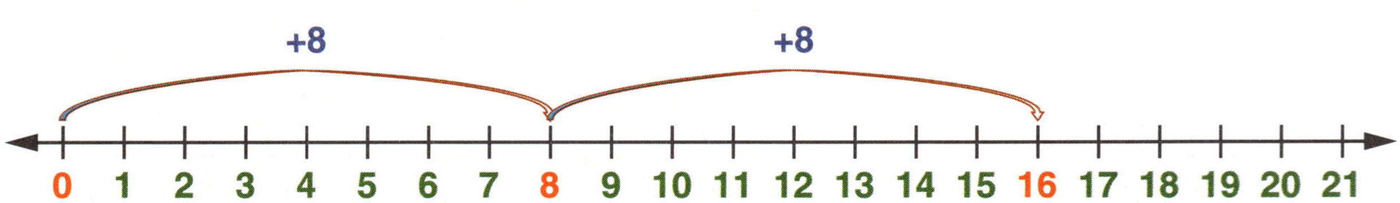

Table of 9

9	1 × 9 = 9
9 + 9	2 × 9 = 18
9 + 9 + 9	3 × 9 = 27
9 + 9 + 9 + 9	4 × 9 = 36
9 + 9 + 9 + 9 + 9	5 × 9 = 45
9 + 9 + 9 + 9 + 9 + 9	6 × 9 = 54
9 + 9 + 9 + 9 + 9 + 9 + 9	7 × 9 = 63
9 + 9 + 9 + 9 + 9 + 9 + 9 + 9	8 × 9 = 72
9 + 9 + 9 + 9 + 9 + 9 + 9 + 9 + 9	9 × 9 = 81
9 + 9 + 9 + 9 + 9 + 9 + 9 + 9 + 9 + 9	10 × 9 = 90

Try These!

1 × 9 = ____

3 × 9 = ____

5 × 9 = ____

7 × 9 = ____

On Number Line

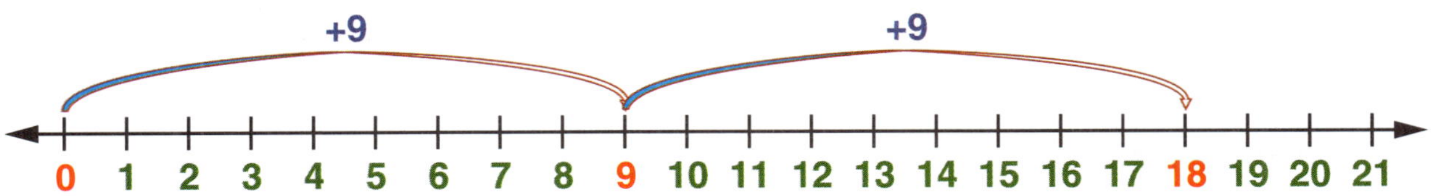

Table of 10

10	1 × 10 = 10
10 + 10	2 × 10 = 20
10 + 10 + 10	3 × 10 = 30
10 + 10 + 10 + 10	4 × 10 = 40
10 + 10 + 10 + 10 + 10	5 × 10 = 50
10 + 10 + 10 + 10 + 10 + 10	6 × 10 = 60
10 + 10 + 10 + 10 + 10 + 10 + 10	7 × 10 = 70
10 + 10 + 10 + 10 + 10 + 10 + 10 + 10	8 × 10 = 80
10 + 10 + 10 + 10 + 10 + 10 + 10 + 10 + 10	9 × 10 = 90
10 + 10 + 10 + 10 + 10 + 10 + 10 + 10 + 10 + 10	10 × 10 = 100

Try These!

1 × 10 = ____

4 × 10 = ____

6 × 10 = ____

8 × 10 = ____

Note

The product of a number and 10 is the same number with a 0 at the end.
The product in the table of 10 always ends with a 0.

On Number Line

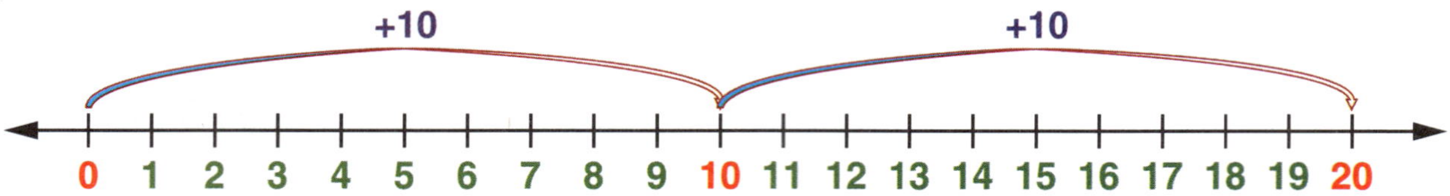

We can multiply using the **Cayley's Table** as given below. If we have to multiply 4 with 5, we look for the number which is placed in the 4th row and in the 5th column, which is 20.

Try These!

Using the Cayley's Table, find the following.

2 × 4 = ____

3 × 5 = ____

1 × 3 = ____

5 × 2 = ____

So, 4 × 5 = 20

×	1	2	3	4	5
1	1	2	3	4	5
2	2	4	6	8	10
3	3	6	9	12	15
4	4	8	12	16	20
5	5	10	15	20	25

Exercise 4.3

Learn all the tables and answer the questions given below.

1. **Fill in the blanks in the given tables.**

Table of 1

1 × 1 = ________

1 × 2 = ________

1 × 3 = ________

1 × 4 = ________

1 × 5 = ________

1 × 6 = ________

1 × 7 = ________

1 × 8 = ________

1 × 9 = ________

1 × 10 = ________

Table of 2

2 × 1 = ________

2 × 2 = ________

2 × 3 = ________

2 × 4 = ________

2 × 5 = ________

2 × 6 = ________

2 × 7 = ________

2 × 8 = ________

2 × 9 = ________

2 × 10 = ________

Table of 3

3 × 1 = ________
3 × 2 = ________
3 × 3 = ________
3 × 4 = ________
3 × 5 = ________
3 × 6 = ________
3 × 7 = ________
3 × 8 = ________
3 × 9 = ________
3 × 10 = ________

Table of 4

4 × 1 = ________
4 × 2 = ________
4 × 3 = ________
4 × 4 = ________
4 × 5 = ________
4 × 6 = ________
4 × 7 = ________
4 × 8 = ________
4 × 9 = ________
4 × 10 = ________

Table of 5

5 × 1 = ________
5 × 2 = ________
5 × 3 = ________
5 × 4 = ________
5 × 5 = ________
5 × 6 = ________
5 × 7 = ________
5 × 8 = ________
5 × 9 = ________
5 × 10 = ________

Table of 6

6 × 1 = ________
6 × 2 = ________
6 × 3 = ________
6 × 4 = ________
6 × 5 = ________
6 × 6 = ________
6 × 7 = ________
6 × 8 = ________
6 × 9 = ________
6 × 10 = ________

Table of 7

7 × 1 = ________
7 × 2 = ________
7 × 3 = ________
7 × 4 = ________
7 × 5 = ________
7 × 6 = ________
7 × 7 = ________
7 × 8 = ________
7 × 9 = ________
7 × 10 = ________

Table of 8

8 × 1 = ________
8 × 2 = ________
8 × 3 = ________
8 × 4 = ________
8 × 5 = ________
8 × 6 = ________
8 × 7 = ________
8 × 8 = ________
8 × 9 = ________
8 × 10 = ________

Table of 9	Table of 10
$9 \times 1 =$ ______	$10 \times 1 =$ ______
$9 \times 2 =$ ______	$10 \times 2 =$ ______
$9 \times 3 =$ ______	$10 \times 3 =$ ______
$9 \times 4 =$ ______	$10 \times 4 =$ ______
$9 \times 5 =$ ______	$10 \times 5 =$ ______
$9 \times 6 =$ ______	$10 \times 6 =$ ______
$9 \times 7 =$ ______	$10 \times 7 =$ ______
$9 \times 8 =$ ______	$10 \times 8 =$ ______
$9 \times 9 =$ ______	$10 \times 9 =$ ______
$9 \times 10 =$ ______	$10 \times 10 =$ ______

2 Fill in the blanks.

a. $2 \times 6 =$ ______ b. $3 \times 2 =$ ______ c. $4 \times 5 =$ ______

d. $5 \times 7 =$ ______ e. $6 \times 3 =$ ______ f. $7 \times 4 =$ ______

g. $8 \times 6 =$ ______ h. $9 \times 2 =$ ______ i. $10 \times 3 =$ ______

j. $2 \times 7 =$ ______ k. $3 \times 8 =$ ______ l. $4 \times 9 =$ ______

m. $5 \times 6 =$ ______ n. $7 \times 8 =$ ______ o. $9 \times 7 =$ ______

3 Fill in the blanks.

a. $2 \times 3 = 3 \times 2 =$ ______ b. $4 \times 5 = 5 \times 4 =$ ______

c. $1 \times 7 = 7 \times 1 =$ ______ d. $3 \times 4 = 4 \times 3 =$ ______

e. $5 \times 6 = 6 \times 5 =$ ______ f. $3 \times 7 = 7 \times 3 =$ ______

Multiplication of 2-digit and 3-digit Numbers by 1-digit Numbers without Carrying

Example 1: Multiply: 12 × 3

We write the multiplication as given below.

	T	O
	1	2
×		3

First, multiply 3 with the 2 in the ones column. That is, 3 × 2 = 6.

We write 6 under 3 in the ones column.

	T	O
	1	2
×		3
	3	6

Next, multiply 3 with 1 in the tens column. That is, 3 × 1 = 3.

We write 3 in the tens column before 6.

Thus, 12 × 3 = 36.

Example 2:

	T	O
	1	4
×		2
	2	8

Thus, 14 × 2 = 28.

Example 3:

	T	O
	1	1
×		6
	6	6

Thus, 11 × 6 = 66.

Special Multiplication

When we multiply a number with a number ending with 0, we can use the short method explained below.

Example

20 × 3

Since 20 has one 0, we write 0 at the end of the answer.

20 × 3 = _0

Next, we multiply 2 by 3.

2 × 3 = 6

So, we write 6 before 0.

20 × 3 = 60

In the same way,

300 × 3 = 900

Example 4: Multiply: 124 × 2

We write the multiplication as given below.

	H	T	O
	1	2	4
×			2
			8

First, multiply 2 by 4 in the ones column. That is, 2 × 4 = 8.

We write 8 in the ones column below 2.

	H	T	O
	1	2	4
×			2
		4	8

Next, multiply 2 by 2 in the tens column. That is, 2 × 2 = 4.

We write 4 in the tens column before 8.

H	T	O
1	2	4
×		2
2	4	8

Then multiply 2 by 1 in the hundreds column. That is, $2 \times 1 = 2$.

We write 2 in the hundreds column before 4.

Thus, $124 \times 2 = 248$.

Remember

Any number multiplied by 0 is 0.

Example 5:

H	T	O
2	3	0
×		3
6	9	0

Thus, $230 \times 3 = 690$.

H	T	O
1	4	3
×		2
2	8	6

Thus, $143 \times 2 = 286$.

Exercise 4.4

1 Multiply the following.

a.

T	O
2	3
×	3

b.

T	O
6	7
×	1

c.

T	O
1	2
×	3

d.

T	O
7	9
×	1

e.

T	O
3	2
×	3

f.

T	O
4	0
×	2

g.

T	O
2	1
×	3

h.

T	O
3	0
×	3

i.

T	O
9	8
×	1

j.

H	T	O
2	1	3
×		3

k.

H	T	O
1	0	4
×		2

l.

H	T	O
9	7	8
×		1

m.

H	T	O
1	0	2
×		4

n.

H	T	O
2	3	1
×		3

o.

H	T	O
6	0	0
×		1

Multiplication of 2-digit and 3-digit Numbers by 1-digit Numbers with Carrying

Example 1: Multiply: 23×4

We will write the multiplication as given below.

T	O
2	3
×	4

First, multiply 4 by 3 in the ones column. That is, $4 \times 3 = 12$.

T	O
$^{1}2$	3
×	4
	2

Write '2' of 12 in the ones column under 4 and carry forward '1' of 12. Write this '1' above 2 in the tens column.

T	O
$^{1}2$	3
×	4
9	2

Now, multiply 4 by 2 in the tens column. That is, $4 \times 2 = 8$.

Add carried forward 1 to 8. That is, $8 + 1 = 9$.

Write 9 in the tens column before 2.

Thus, $23 \times 4 = 92$.

Example 2:

T	O
$^{3}3$	5
×	6
2 1	0

Thus, $35 \times 6 = 210$.

Example 3:

T	O
$^{1}7$	4
×	3
2 2	2

Thus, $74 \times 3 = 222$.

Example 4: Multiply: 314×3

H	T	O
3	$^{1}1$	4
×		3
		2

Multiply 3 by 4 in the ones column.
That is, $3 \times 4 = 12$.

Write '2' of 12 in ones column under 3 and carry forward '1' of 12 to the tens column above 1.

H	T	O
3	$^{1}1$	4
×		3
	4	2

Now, multiply 3 by 1 in the tens column. That is, $3 \times 1 = 3$.

To this 3, add the 1 that was carried forward.
That is, $3 + 1 = 4$.

Write 4 in the tens column before 2.

H	T	O
3	$^{1}1$	4
×		3
9	4	2

Now, multiply 3 by 3 in the hundreds column.
That is, $3 \times 3 = 9$.

Write 9 in the hundreds column before 4.

Thus, $314 \times 3 = 942$.

Example 5:

H	T	O
$^{1}2$	$^{1}3$	3
×		4
9	3	2

Thus, $233 \times 4 = 932$.

Example 6:

H	T	O
1	$^{1}0$	3
×		5
5	1	5

Thus, $103 \times 5 = 515$.

Exercise 4.5

1 **Multiply the following.**

	T	O
a.	1	2
	×	5
b.	3	6
	×	4
c.	7	3
	×	6
d.	2	5
	×	6
e.	4	3
	×	5
f.	4	7
	×	2
g.	4	5
	×	3
h.	8	4
	×	7
i.	7	4
	×	3
j.	8	2
	×	7
k.	2	8
	×	3
l.	6	2
	×	5
m.	9	2
	×	8
n.	6	9
	×	2
o.	9	5
	×	2

2 **Multiply the following.**

	H	T	O
a.	2	4	5
	×		4
b.	1	5	3
	×		6
c.	2	7	4
	×		3
d.	1	4	3
	×		6
e.	1	4	6
	×		5
f.	2	5	6
	×		2
g.	3	2	7
	×		3
h.	2	3	5
	×		4
i.	3	0	6
	×		3

j.

H	T	O
2	1	3
×		4

k.

H	T	O
2	6	5
×		3

l.

H	T	O
2	2	8
×		2

m.

H	T	O
2	3	9
×		3

n.

H	T	O
4	9	6
×		2

o.

H	T	O
3	5	8
×		2

Word Problems

In word problems, whenever the answer increases, we add or multiply.

When the answer increases exactly by the number given in the question, we **add**.

When the answer increases many times the number given in the question, we **multiply**.

When the value of one item is given and we have to find the value of more items, we **multiply**.

Word Problems Involving Smaller Numbers

Example 1: In a classroom, 8 children sit in 1 row. How many children sit in 4 rows?

Number of children in one row = 8

Number of children in 4 rows = $4 \times 8 = 32$

Thus, 32 children sit in 4 rows.

Example 2: There are 6 pencils in 1 box. How many pencils are there in 9 such boxes?

Number of pencils in one box = 6

Number of pencils in 9 boxes = $9 \times 6 = 54$

Thus, there are 54 pencils in 9 boxes.

Exercise 4.6

1. One tricycle has 3 wheels. How many wheels are there in 7 tricycles?

Number of wheels in one tricycle = ________

Number of wheels in 7 tricycles = ________ × ________

= ________

There are ________ wheels in 7 tricycles.

2. One packet has 4 sandwiches. How many sandwiches are there in 6 packets?

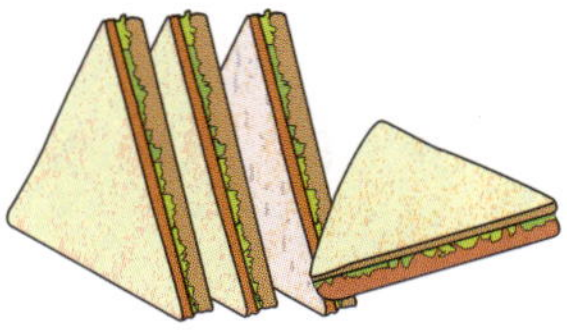

There are ________ sandwiches in 6 packets.

3. 1 car has 4 wheels. How many wheels are there in 8 cars?

There are ________ wheels in 8 cars.

4. A book has 10 pages. Each page has 2 pictures. What is the total number of pictures? (Hint: Each means 'one'.)

There are ________ pictures in total.

5. In one kilogram, you get 7 oranges. How many oranges will you get in 6 kilograms?

There will be ________ oranges in 6 kilograms.

6. One cake can be cut into 4 pieces. How many pieces can you get out of 7 cakes?

We get ________ pieces out of 7 cakes.

Word Problems Involving Bigger Numbers

Example 3: There are 30 chairs in one classroom, how many chairs will be there in 5 classrooms?

	T	O
	3	0
	×	5
1	5	0

Number of chairs in one classroom = 30

Number of chairs in 5 classrooms = 30×5

Thus, 5 classrooms will have 150 chairs.

Example 4: A baker sells 125 cakes in one day. How many cakes does he sell in 2 days?

H	T	O
1	[1]2	5
×		2
2	5	0

Number of cakes sold by the baker in 1 day = 125

Number of cakes sold by the baker in 2 days = 125×2

Thus, in 2 days, the baker sells 250 cakes.

Example 5: If a fruit vendor sells 50 apples in one day, how many apples does he sell in 6 days?

	T	O
	5	0
	×	6
3	0	0

Number of apples sold by the vendor in 1 day = 50

Number of apples sold by the vendor in 6 days = 50×6

Thus, vendor will sell 300 apples in 6 days.

Exercise 4.7

1. 53 people can sit in one bus. How many people can sit in 3 buses?

Thus, ________ can sit in 3 buses.

2. Ram earns ₹148 in one day. How much money does he earn in 2 days?

Thus, Ram earns ₹________ in 2 days.

3. 250 people can sit in one aeroplane. How many people can sit in 3 aeroplanes?

Thus, ________ people can sit in 3 aeroplanes.

4. There are 112 colour pencils in one packet. How many colour pencils are there in 5 packets?

Thus, ________ pencils are there in 5 packets.

5. One box has 126 pieces of chocolates. How many pieces of chocolates are there in 3 boxes?

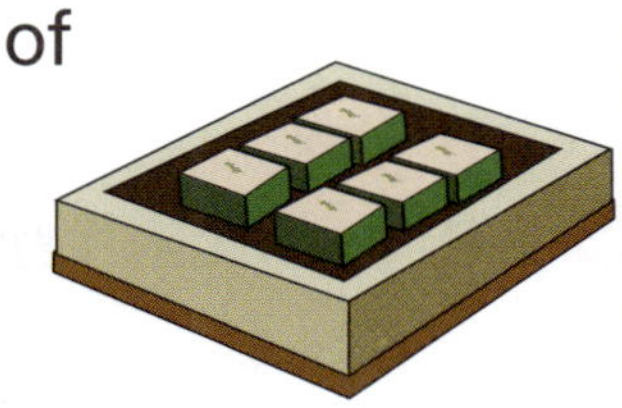

Thus, ________ pieces of chocolates are there in 3 boxes.

For the Curious Mind

If $4 \times 2 = 8$

$4 \times 20 = 80$

$4 \times 20 = 800$

then, $4 \times 2000 =$ ________

$4 \times 20000 =$ ________

Revision Exercise

1 Fill in the blanks.

In $2 \times 9 = 18$,

the multiplier is ______ .

the multiplicand is ______ .

the product is ______ .

2 Fill in the blanks.

a. $3 \times 6 =$ ______ $\times 3$

b. $4 \times 8 = 8 \times$ ______

c. $9 \times 1 =$ ______

d. $9 \times 0 =$ ______

3 Fill in the blanks.

a. $3 \times 5 =$ ______

b. $6 \times 8 =$ ______

c. $9 \times 3 =$ ______

d. $4 \times 3 =$ ______

e. $7 \times 4 =$ ______

f. $8 \times 3 =$ ______

4 Fill in the blanks.

a. $20 \times 3 =$ ______

b. $50 \times 6 =$ ______

c. $400 \times 2 =$ ______

5 Solve the following.

a.

	T	O
	1	3
×		2

b.

	T	O
	3	4
×		6

c.

	H	T	O
	1	2	3
×			2

d.

	H	T	O
	2	4	2
×			4

6 One child eats 5 ice creams. How many ice creams will 7 children eat?

Thus, 7 children will eat ______ ice creams.

7 A teacher checks 105 notebooks in one day. How many notebooks does she check in 5 days?

Thus, the teacher checks ______ notebooks in 5 days.

Mixed Review 1

1 Fill in the blanks.

a.

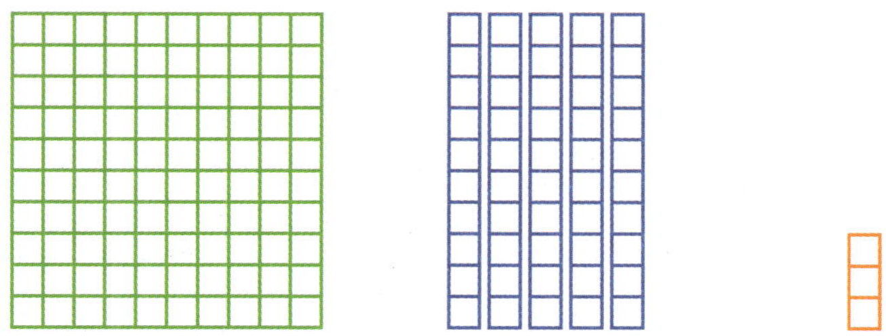

_____ hundreds _____ tens _____ ones

Number name = ____________________

2 Fill in the blanks.

a. 889 = _____ hundreds _____ tens _____ ones

Number name = ____________________

b. 148 = _____ hundreds _____ tens _____ ones

Number name = ____________________

3 Fill in the blanks with >, < or =.

a. 778 _____ 887

b. 567 _____ 576

4 Fill in the blanks.

4 + 2 = _____

40 + 20 = _____

400 + 200 = _____

5 Add the following.

a.

	H	T	O
	6	2	3
+	1	6	4

b.

	H	T	O
	3	9	2
+		4	8

c.

	H	T	O
	7	0	0
+	1	0	0

d.

	T	O
	2	1
	3	2
+	1	4

e.

	T	O
	2	4
	3	5
+	1	6

f.

	H	T	O
	1	4	2
	2	0	3
+	5	5	1

6 **Subtract the following.**

a. 7 – 2 = ______ 70 – 20 = ______ 700 – 200 = ______

7 **Subtract the following:**

a.

	H	T	O
	7	5	4
–	6	2	3

b.

	H	T	O
	9	4	7
–		1	3

c.

	H	T	O
	4	3	2
–			1

d.

	H	T	O
	9	8	3
–	6	4	5

8 **Multiply the following.**

a. 4 × 7 = ______ b. 8 × 3 = ______ c. 9 × 2 = ______

d. 6 × 5 = ______ e. 20 × 4 = ______ f. 50 × 7 = ______

g. 300 × 2 = ______ h. 700 × 1 = ______ i. 400 × 2 = ______

9 **Multiply:**

3 × 2 = ______ 3 × 20 = ______ 3 × 200 = ______

10 **Multiply:**

a.

	T	O
	1	2
×		4

b.

	T	O
	2	5
×		4

c.

	H	T	O
	3	2	1
×			3

d.

	H	T	O
	1	2	5
×			3

e.

	H	T	O
	1	6	7
×			5

11 **In a movie hall, there were 47 men, 65 women and 20 children. How many people were there in the movie hall?**

There were ______ people in the movie hall.

12 **A fruitseller had 235 apples. He sold 199 apples in one day. How many apples were left with him?**

Thus, _____ apples were left with him.

13. **159 people went to the circus in the morning. 99 more people went to the circus in the afternoon. 140 people left the circus by the evening. How many people were at the circus in the evening?**

Thus, ______ people were at the circus in the evening.

14. **One storybook costs ₹75. How much will 3 storybooks cost?**

Thus, three storybooks will cost ______.

15. **A shopkeeper sells 250 coconuts in one month. How many coconuts will he sell in 3 months?**

The shopkeeper will sell ______ coconuts in 3 months.

16. **A bookseller sells 140 copies of a book every day. How many copies of the book will she sell in a week?**

Thus, the bookseller sells ______copies in a week.

Division

5

Let us revise what we learned about division in Class 1 and learn more about division of numbers.

Let's Get Started

1. We learned in Class 1 that division is repeated subtraction.

   Fill in the blanks based on repeated subtraction.

   15 ÷ 3 = ____ 15 – ____ – ____ – ____ – ____ – ____ = 0

   Here, 3 is subtracted ____ times from 15 to get 0, so 15 ÷ 3 = ____.

2. We learned to represent division of numbers on a number line.

   Show 14 ÷ 2 on the number line.

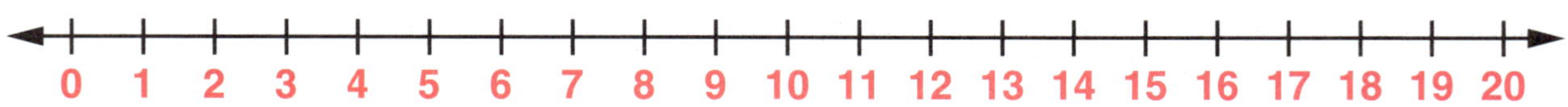

3. Division is also used when we have to share something equally.

   Share 6 sweets equally among 3 children.

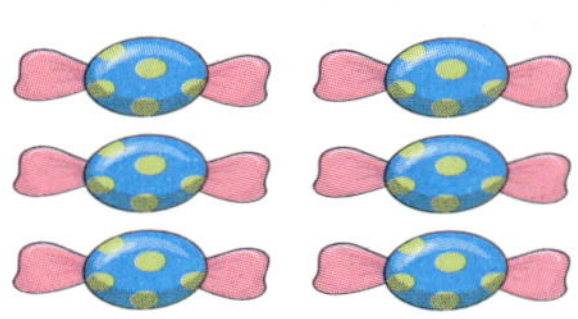

   We find that each child gets ____ sweets.

Relation between Multiplication and Division

Consider that we have to make 4 groups of 2 cherries each.

Then we will have 8 cherries in total.

This can be represented as $4 \times 2 = 8$.

Again, consider that we have to group 8 cherries into groups of 2.

Then we will have 4 groups as shown above.

This can be represented as $8 \div 2 = 4$.

Therefore, we can conclude that if we have $4 \times 2 = 8$, then we have $8 \div 2 = 4$ and $8 \div 4 = 2$.

Similarly, if $3 \times 4 = 12$, then, $12 \div 3 = 4$ and $12 \div 4 = 3$.

Multiplication tables help in finding the answer to division problems.

For example, solve $16 \div 2$.

We can use the table of 2. Write the table of 2 till the product reaches 16.

$1 \times 2 = 1$	$5 \times 2 = 10$
$2 \times 2 = 4$	$6 \times 2 = 12$
$3 \times 2 = 6$	$7 \times 2 = 14$
$4 \times 2 = 8$	$8 \times 2 = $ (16)

Therefore, $16 \div 2 = \underline{8}$.

Remember

Dividend: The number we are dividing is the dividend.
Divisor: The number by which we are dividing is the divisor.
Quotient: The number we get as the answer is the quotient.
For example, in $6 \div 2 = 3$, 6 is the dividend, 2 is the divisor and 3 is the quotient.

Exercise 5.1

1 Solve the following.

a. If $3 \times 4 = 12$,
then $12 \div 3 = $ ____
and $12 \div 4 = $ ____.

b. If $6 \times 3 = 18$,
then $18 \div 6 = $ ____
and $18 \div 3 = $ ____.

c. If $7 \times 4 = 28$,
then $28 \div 7 = $ ____
and $28 \div 4 = $ ____.

d. If $8 \times 9 = 72$,
then $72 \div 8 = $ ____
and $72 \div 9 = $ ____.

e. If $5 \times 7 = 35$,
then $35 \div 5 =$ ____
and $35 \div 7 =$ ____.

f. If $2 \times 9 = 18$,
then $18 \div 2 =$ ____
and $18 \div 9 =$ ____.

2 Fill in the blanks.

a. If $14 \div 7 = 2$, then $2 \times 7 =$ ____.

b. If $36 \div 6 = 6$, then $6 \times 6 =$ ____.

c. If $63 \div 7 = 9$, then $9 \times 7 =$ ____.

d. If $24 \div 4 = 6$, then $6 \times 4 =$ ____.

3 Use the multiplication tables to solve the following.

a. $6 \div 3 =$ ____ b. $12 \div 4 =$ ____ c. $20 \div 2 =$ ____ d. $32 \div 8 =$ ____

Division by 1-digit Numbers without Remainder

Remember

Division Facts

1. If we divide a number by 1, we get the same number as the quotient.
2. If we divide 0 by any number, we get 0 as the quotient.
3. If we divide a number by itself, we get 1 as the quotient.

Short Division

We can solve division problems by the short division method as explained below.

Example 1: Divide 8 by 2 using short division method.

```
               2 | 8   ← Write the dividend here.
Write the  →     ---
divisor here.     4    ← Write the quotient here.
```

Example 2: Divide 10 by 5 using short division method.

```
5 | 10
  ----
    2    Quotient = 2
```

Exercise 5.2

Solve the following by short division. Two have been done for you.

1. $6 \div 2$

   2 | 6   Quotient = 3

2. $8 \div 2$

   2 | 8   Quotient = 4

③ $10 \div 5$ $5 \,\lfloor\, 10$ Quotient = _____	④ $12 \div 2$ $2 \,\lfloor\, 12$ Quotient = _____	⑤ $16 \div 2$ $2 \,\lfloor\, 16$ Quotient = _____	⑥ $15 \div 5$ $5 \,\lfloor\, 15$ Quotient = _____
⑦ $18 \div 2$ $2 \,\lfloor\, 18$ Quotient = _____	⑧ $25 \div 5$ $5 \,\lfloor\, 25$ Quotient = _____	⑨ $4 \div 2$ $2 \,\lfloor\, 4$ Quotient = _____	⑩ $14 \div 2$ $2 \,\lfloor\, 14$ Quotient = _____

Long Division

Let us learn a new method to divide.

Example 3: Divide: $6 \div 2$

We write long division as shown with the dividend inside and the divisor outside.

$$2\overline{)6}$$

We have to find out how many times 2 is contained in 6. The multiplication table tells us that $2 \times 3 = 6$

Therefore, $6 \div 2 = 3$.

This means that 2 is contained 3 times in 6.

$$\textcircled{2} \times 3 = \textcircled{6}$$

3 ↓ Quotient

So, in long division, we write 3 times 2 is equal to 6 as shown below.

$$\begin{array}{r} 3 \\ 2\overline{)6} \\ -6 \\ \hline 0 \end{array}$$

0 ← Remainder

Now, we draw a line below the second 6 and subtract 6 from 6, which is equal to 0.

We write 0 below the line.

Remember

The number that is left after division is the remainder.

Thus, $6 \div 2 = 3$.

While dividing, if the first digit is smaller than the divisor, then we take the first two digits and divide them by the divisor. Look at the example.

$$\begin{array}{r} 4 \\ 3\overline{)12} \\ -12 \\ \hline 0 \end{array}$$

Therefore, $12 \div 3 = 4$.

Exercise 5.3

Solve the following by long division.

1. $6 \div 2$

   $2\overline{)6}$

   $6 \div 2 =$ ____

2. $10 \div 2$

   $2\overline{)10}$

   $10 \div 2 =$ ____

3. $15 \div 3$

   $3\overline{)15}$

   $15 \div 3 =$ ____

4. $18 \div 9$

   $9\overline{)18}$

   $18 \div 9 =$ ____

5. $24 \div 6$

   $6\overline{)24}$

   $24 \div 6 =$ ____

6. $14 \div 7$

   $7\overline{)14}$

   $14 \div 7 =$ ____

7. $12 \div 2$

   $2\overline{)12}$

   $12 \div 2 =$ ____

8. $32 \div 8$

   $8\overline{)32}$

   $32 \div 8 =$ ____

9. $30 \div 5$

   $5\overline{)30}$

   $30 \div 5 =$ ____

Understanding Remainder

In division, we group the objects equally. Sometimes, we are unable to group the objects equally and we are left with some objects. The leftover is known as the remainder. For example, group 5 ice creams into 2 groups.

After grouping, we are left with 1 ice cream.

Hence, 1 is the leftover here, which is the remainder.

5 ÷ 2 gives 2 as the quotient and 1 as the remainder.

Division by 1-digit Numbers with Remainder

Example 1: Divide: $7 \div 2$

We write the long division as shown here. $2\overline{)7}$

Find out how many times 2 is contained in 7. Recall the table of 2.

We find that $3 \times 2 = 6$ (which is smaller than 7)

and $4 \times 2 = 8$ (which is greater than 7)

Since 8 is greater than 7, we will use $3 \times 2 = 6$, which is smaller than 7.

$$\begin{array}{r} 3 \\ 2\overline{)7} \\ -6 \\ \hline 1 \end{array}$$

Write 6 below 7 and subtract. We get 3 as the quotient and 1 as the remainder.

Thus, quotient = 3 and remainder = 1.

Example 2: Divide: $13 \div 5$

We write the division as shown here: $5\overline{)13}$

We have to now find out how many times 5 is contained in 13.

Let us recall the table of 5.

$2 \times 5 = 10$ (which is smaller than 13)

$3 \times 5 = 15$ (which is greater than 13)

So, we will use $5 \times 2 = 10$.

$$\begin{array}{r} 2 \\ 5\overline{)13} \\ -10 \\ \hline 3 \end{array}$$

Write 10 below 13 and subtract. We get 2 as the quotient and 3 as the remainder.

Thus, quotient = 2 and remainder = 3.

Exercise 5.4

Solve the following using long division.

1. $5 \div 2$

   $2\overline{)5}$

   − ___

   Quotient = _____

   Remainder = _____

2. $12 \div 7$

   $7\overline{)12}$

   − ___

   Quotient = _____

   Remainder = _____

3. $9 \div 2$

   $2\overline{)9}$

   − ___

   Quotient = _____

   Remainder = _____

4. $21 \div 6$

   $6\overline{)21}$

   − ___

   Quotient = _____

   Remainder = _____

5. $11 \div 8$

   $8\overline{)11}$

   − ___

   Quotient = _____

   Remainder = _____

6. $19 \div 4$

   $4\overline{)19}$

   − ___

   Quotient = _____

   Remainder = _____

7 $18 \div 5$

$5\overline{)18}$

$-$ ___

Quotient = ____

Remainder = ____

8 $13 \div 2$

$2\overline{)13}$

$-$ ___

Quotient = ____

Remainder = ____

9 $26 \div 7$

$7\overline{)26}$

$-$ ___

Quotient = ____

Remainder = ____

Division Involving 2-digit Quotient

Without Remainder

Let us learn to solve division problems where we get 2-digit quotient.

Example 1: Divide 68 by 2.

We will write the division problem as given below.

$2\overline{)68}$ Take the first digit of 68, which is 6. We divide it by 2.

$$\begin{array}{r} 3 \\ 2\overline{)68} \\ -6 \\ \hline 0 \end{array}$$

$3 \times 2 = 6$

$\therefore 6 \div 2 = 3$

We write 3 in the quotient place, 6 below 6 and subtract.

We draw a line below 6 and write 0 below the line.

$$\begin{array}{r} 34 \\ 2\overline{)68} \\ -6\downarrow \\ \hline 08 \\ -8 \\ \hline 0 \end{array}$$

We bring 8 down and write it next to 0.

Now, we divide 8 by 2.

$4 \times 2 = 8$

$\therefore 8 \div 2 = 4$

We write 4 in the quotient place next to 3 and 8 under 8.

Draw a line under 8 and subtract.

We get 0 as the remainder and 34 as the quotient.

Therefore, $68 \div 2 = 34$.

Thus, quotient = 34 and remainder = 0.

With Remainder

Example 2: Divide: $35 \div 2$

We will write the question as given below.

$$2\overline{)35}$$

$$\begin{array}{r} 1 \\ 2\overline{)35} \\ -2 \\ \hline 15 \end{array}$$

First divide 3 by 2.

$1 \times 2 = 2 \quad 2 \times 2 = 4$

We will use $1 \times 2 = 2$.

$3 - 2 = 1$

Bring down 5.

$$\begin{array}{r} 17 \\ 2\overline{)35} \\ -2 \\ \hline 15 \\ -14 \\ \hline 1 \end{array}$$

Now, divide 15 by 2.

$7 \times 2 = 14 \quad 8 \times 2 = 16$

We will use $7 \times 2 = 14$.

$15 - 14 = 1$

Remainder will be 1.

Thus, quotient = 17 and remainder = 1.

If the Last Digit of the Divisor is 0

Example 1: Divide: $40 \div 2$

We will write the question as shown below.

$$2\overline{)40}$$

$$\begin{array}{r} 2 \\ 2\overline{)40} \\ -4 \\ \hline 0 \end{array}$$

We will first divide the first digit of 40, which is 4.

Since $2 \times 2 = 4$

$\therefore 4 \div 2 = 2$.

We write 2 in the quotient place and 4 below 4. Draw a line below 4 and subtract. $4 - 4 = 0$.

Write 0 below 4.

$$\begin{array}{r} 20 \\ 2\overline{)40} \\ -4 \\ \hline 00 \end{array}$$

Now, bring down the 0 of 40

Since we have 0 which is smaller than the divisor, we will write a 0 in the quotient next to 2.

Thus, quotient = 20 and remainder = 0.

Note

After bringing down a number, if the number to be divided is smaller than the divisor or it is 0, then we add 0 to the quotient.

Exercise 5.5

Solve the following using long division. Write the Quotient (Q), Remainder (R).

1. $64 \div 2$

$2\overline{)64}$

Q = ______

R = ______

2. $46 \div 3$

$3\overline{)46}$

Q = ______

R = ______

3. $62 \div 5$

$5\overline{)62}$

Q = ______

R = ______

4 $77 \div 6$ $6\overline{)77}$ Q = ____ R = ____	5 $84 \div 7$ $7\overline{)84}$ Q = ____ R = ____	6 $93 \div 8$ $8\overline{)93}$ Q = ____ R = ____
7 $62 \div 2$ $2\overline{)62}$ Q = ____ R = ____	8 $51 \div 3$ $3\overline{)51}$ Q = ____ R = ____	9 $40 \div 4$ $4\overline{)40}$ Q = ____ R = ____
10 $67 \div 4$ $4\overline{)67}$ Q = ____ R = ____	11 $72 \div 5$ $5\overline{)72}$ Q = ____ R = ____	12 $81 \div 6$ $6\overline{)81}$ Q = ____ R = ____
13 $93 \div 7$ $7\overline{)93}$ Q = ____ R = ____	14 $99 \div 8$ $8\overline{)99}$ Q = ____ R = ____	15 $59 \div 6$ $6\overline{)59}$ Q = ____ R = ____

Revision Exercise

1 Fill in the blanks.

a. If $5 \times 6 = 30$,
then $30 \div 5 =$ ____
and $30 \div 6 =$ ____.

b. If $7 \times 3 = 21$,
then $21 \div 7 =$ ____
and $21 \div 3 =$ ____.

2 Fill in the blanks.

a. If $28 \div 7 = 4$, then $7 \times 4 =$ ____.

b. If $27 \div 9 = 3$, then $9 \times 3 =$ ____.

3 Use multiplication to solve the following.

a. $4 \div 2 =$ ____

b. $16 \div 4 =$ ____

4 Solve the following by short division.

a. $20 \div 5$

5 | 20

Quotient = ____

b. $18 \div 2$

2 | 18

Quotient = ____

5 Solve the following by long division.

a. $12 \div 2 =$

2) 1 2

Quotient = ____

b. $25 \div 5 =$

5) 2 5

Quotient = ____

c. $21 \div 7 =$

7) 2 1

Quotient = ____

d. $36 \div 9 =$

9) 3 6

Quotient = ____

6 Solve the following using long division.

a. $7 \div 2$

2) 7

−

Quotient = ____
Remainder = ____

b. $15 \div 4$

4) 1 5

−

Quotient = ____
Remainder = ____

c. $5 \div 3$

$3\overline{)5}$
$-$ ___

Quotient = _____
Remainder = _____

d. $17 \div 6$

$6\overline{)17}$
$-$ ___

Quotient = _____
Remainder = _____

7 Solve the following using long division.

a. $56 \div 2$

$2\overline{)56}$

Quotient = _____
Remainder = _____

b. $99 \div 3$

$3\overline{)99}$

Quotient = _____
Remainder = _____

c. $78 \div 5$

$5\overline{)78}$

Quotient = _____
Remainder = _____

d. $77 \div 6$

$6\overline{)77}$

Quotient = _____
Remainder = _____

e. $99 \div 2$

$2\overline{)99}$

Quotient = _____
Remainder = _____

f. $46 \div 8$

$8\overline{)46}$

Quotient = _____
Remainder = _____

g. $79 \div 6$

$6\overline{)79}$

Quotient = _____
Remainder = _____

h. $50 \div 5$

$5\overline{)50}$

Quotient = _____
Remainder = _____

Worksheet

1 **Write the multiplication and division facts for these numbers. One has been done for you.**

24 (4, 6)	35 (7, 5)	36 (9, 4)
4 × 6 = 24	___ × ___ = ___	___ × ___ = ___
6 × 4 = 24	___ × ___ = ___	___ × ___ = ___
24 ÷ 4 = 6	___ ÷ ___ = ___	___ ÷ ___ = ___
24 ÷ 6 = 4	___ ÷ ___ = ___	___ ÷ ___ = ___

2 **Divide the following and match each quotient with its remainder.**

	No remainder	
78 ÷ 5	1	86 ÷ 9
	2	
61 ÷ 3	3	92 ÷ 8
	4	
84 ÷ 4	5	74 ÷ 6

For the Curious Mind

Fill in the boxes. One has been done for you.

30 → ÷3 → 10; ÷5 → ___

40 → ÷2 → ___; ÷4 → ___

50 → ÷5 → ___; ÷10 → ___

More on Division

6

In this chapter, let us learn to divide bigger numbers.

Division of 3-digit Numbers by 1-digit Numbers

Without Remainder

Example 1: Divide: $264 \div 2$

We will solve this by long division. We will write the question as shown below.

$$2\overline{)264}$$

Take the first digit of 264, which is 2. Divide it by 2.

$$\begin{array}{r} 1 \\ 2\overline{)264} \\ -2 \\ \hline 0 \end{array}$$

$1 \times 2 = 2$ So, $2 \div 2 = 1$.

We write 1 in the quotient and 2 below 2. Draw a line under 2 and subtract. $2 - 2 = 0$.

We write 0 below the line.

$$\begin{array}{r} 13 \\ 2\overline{)264} \\ -2\downarrow \\ \hline 06 \\ -6 \\ \hline 0 \end{array}$$

We bring down 6 and write it next to 0. Now, we divide 6 by 2.

$3 \times 2 = 6$ So, $6 \div 2 = 3$.

We write 3 in the quotient next to 1 and 6 under 6. Draw a line under 6 and subtract. $6 - 6 = 0$.

We write 0 under the line.

$$\begin{array}{r} 132 \\ 2\overline{)264} \\ -2\downarrow \\ \hline 06 \\ -6\downarrow \\ \hline 04 \\ -4 \\ \hline 0 \end{array}$$

Now, we bring down 4.

Divide 4 by 2.

$2 \times 2 = 4$ So, $4 \div 2 = 2$.

We write 2 in the quotient next to 3 and 4 under 4. Draw a line under 4 and subtract. $4 - 4 = 0$.

We write 0 under the line.

Thus, $264 \div 2 = 132$.

With Remainder

Example 2: Divide: $126 \div 4$

When the first digit of the dividend is smaller than the divisor, we divide the first two digits together.

$$\begin{array}{r} 3 \\ 4\overline{)126} \\ -12\downarrow \\ \hline 06 \end{array}$$

Since the first digit 1 is smaller than the divisor, we take the first two digits together and divide. So, we divide 12 by 4.

$3 \times 4 = 12.$

$\therefore$ We write 3 in the quotient and 12 below 12. Draw a line below 12 and subtract. $12 - 12 = 0$

Write 0 below 12 and bring down 6.

$$\begin{array}{r} 31 \\ 4\overline{)126} \\ -12\downarrow \\ \hline 06 \\ -4 \\ \hline 2 \end{array}$$

Now, we divide 6 by 4.

$1 \times 4 = 4$

$2 \times 4 = 8$

Since 8 is greater than 6, we write 1 in the quotient and 4 below 6. Draw a line below 4 and subtract. $6 - 4 = 2$

Thus, quotient = 31 and remainder = 2.

When Dividend has 0 in it

Example 3: Divide: $402 \div 2$

We will write the question as shown below.

$$2\overline{)402}$$

Take the first digit of 402, which is 4.

$$\begin{array}{r} 2 \\ 2\overline{)402} \\ -4\downarrow \\ \hline 00 \end{array}$$

Divide it by 2.

$2 \times 2 = 4$

$\therefore 4 \div 2 = 2$

We write 2 in the quotient and 4 below 4, and subtract.

We draw a line below 4 and write 0 below the line.

Now, bring down the next digit of 402, which is 0.

$$\begin{array}{r} 201 \\ 2\overline{)402} \\ -4\downarrow\downarrow \\ \hline 002 \\ -2 \\ \hline 0 \end{array}$$

Since we have 00 and that cannot be divided by 2, we write 0 in the quotient and bring down the last digit, which is 2.

Now, divide 2 by 2. $1 \times 2 = 2$

So, $2 \div 2 = 1.$

Write 1 in the quotient and 2 below 2. Draw a line below 2 and subtract. $2 - 2 = 0.$

Thus, $402 \div 2 = 201.$

Example 4: Divide: 360 ÷ 3

$$\begin{array}{r} 120 \\ 3\overline{)360} \\ -3\downarrow \\ \hline 06 \\ -6\downarrow \\ \hline 00 \end{array}$$

Take the first digit of 360, which is 3. Divide it by 3.

$1 \times 3 = 3$ Therefore, $3 \div 1 = 3$,

We write 1 in the quotient, 3 below 3 and subtract. $3 - 3 = 0$.

Bring down the next digit that is 6 below.

Now, $2 \times 3 = 6$, Therefore, $6 \div 2 = 3$.

We write 2 in the quotient, 6 below 6 and subtract. $6 - 6 = 0$.

When we bring the last digit down, we get 00, which is smaller than the divisor 3. So, we add a 0 in the quotient next to 2.

Thus, $360 \div 3 = 120$.

Exercise 6.1

Solve the following by long division. Write the Quotient (Q), Remainder (R).

1. 842 ÷ 4 — $4\overline{)842}$ Q = ____ R = ____
2. 369 ÷ 3 — $3\overline{)369}$ Q = ____ R = ____
3. 488 ÷ 4 — $4\overline{)488}$ Q = ____ R = ____
4. 366 ÷ 6 — $6\overline{)366}$ Q = ____ R = ____
5. 452 ÷ 3 — $3\overline{)452}$ Q = ____ R = ____
6. 554 ÷ 5 — $5\overline{)554}$ Q = ____ R = ____
7. 408 ÷ 4 — $4\overline{)408}$ Q = ____ R = ____
8. 930 ÷ 3 — $3\overline{)930}$ Q = ____ R = ____
9. 488 ÷ 4 — $4\overline{)488}$ Q = ____ R = ____
10. 729 ÷ 6 — $6\overline{)729}$ Q = ____ R = ____
11. 578 ÷ 5 — $5\overline{)578}$ Q = ____ R = ____
12. 497 ÷ 7 — $7\overline{)497}$ Q = ____ R = ____

Word Problems on Division

We have solved some problems on division in Class 1.

Some Points to Remember

1. We subtract when the answer reduces exactly by the quantity given in the question.
2. We divide when something has to be shared or distributed equally.
3. We divide when the value of many quantities is given and we have to find the value of 1 quantity.

Example 1: 12 sandwiches have to be shared equally among 6 boys. How many sandwiches will each boy get?

Number of sandwiches = 12

Number of boys = 6

$$12 \div 6 = \begin{array}{r} 2 \\ 6\overline{)12} \\ -12 \\ \hline 0 \end{array}$$

Thus, each boy will get 2 sandwiches.

Note

Since the problem involves equal sharing, we will divide. The bigger number will always be the dividend and the smaller number will be the divisor. When we solve this question, we will write statements as shown.

Example 2: 3 boys can sit on one bench. How many benches do we need for 18 boys?

Number of boys = 18

Number of benches = 3

$$18 \div 3 = \begin{array}{r} 6 \\ 3\overline{)18} \\ -18 \\ \hline 0 \end{array}$$

Thus, we need 6 benches.

Note

Since the boys will be sharing the benches, we will divide.

Note

Whenever we have to distribute, we divide.

Example 3: 54 cookies are distributed among 9 children. How many cookies will each child get?

Number of cookies = 54

Number of children = 9

$$54 \div 9 = \begin{array}{r} 6 \\ 9\overline{)54} \\ -54 \\ \hline 0 \end{array}$$

Thus, each child will get 6 cookies.

Note

When we have to find the value of **one** or **each**, we divide.

Example 4: If you distribute 20 *samosas* among 6 girls, how many *samosas* will each girl get and how many *samosas* will be left?

Number of *samosas* = 20

Number of girls = 6

$$\begin{array}{r} 3 \\ 6\overline{)20} \\ -18 \\ \hline 2 \end{array}$$

3 ⟶ *samosas* each girl gets

2 ⟶ *samosas* left

Note

The remainder is always what is left.

Thus, each girl will get 3 *samosas* and 2 *samosas* will be left.

Exercise 6.2

1. 24 chocolates have to be shared equally among 6 children. How many chocolates will each child get?

   Number of chocolates = ______

   Number of children = ______

   $6\overline{)24}$

   24 ÷ 6 = ______

   Each child will get ______ chocolates.

2. 48 children travel to school by car. 4 children can sit in 1 car. In how many cars do the children travel?

48 children travel in ______ cars.

3. Distribute 18 pencils among 9 children. How many pencils will each child get?

Each child will get ______ pencils.

4. 23 children are asked to stand in 3 lines. How many children will stand in a line? How many children will be left out?

There will be ______ children in a line. ______ will be left out.

5. 16 flower saplings have to be planted in 8 pots. How many saplings will be planted in each pot?

______ saplings will be planted in each pot.

6 95 people have to travel by bus from Delhi to Agra. There are 5 buses. How many people will sit in each bus?

______ people will sit in each bus.

7 ₹150 is divided equally among 3 people. How much does each person get?

Each person gets ₹ ______.

8 730 people sit in 5 different movie halls. Each movie hall has an equal number of people. How many people are there in each movie hall?

______ people are there in each movie hall.

9 23 children want to play cricket. There can be only 2 teams. How many children will there be in each team? How many will be left?

There will be ______ children in each team.

______ will be left.

Revision Exercise

1 **Solve the following by long division.**

a. 154 ÷ 7

$7\overline{)154}$

Quotient = _____
Remainder = _____

b. 660 ÷ 6

$6\overline{)660}$

Quotient = _____
Remainder = _____

c. 204 ÷ 4

$4\overline{)204}$

Quotient = _____
Remainder = _____

d. 800 ÷ 8

$8\overline{)800}$

Quotient = _____
Remainder = _____

2 Distribute 729 coloured pencils among 9 girls. How many coloured pencils will each girl get?

Each girl will get ______ coloured pencils.

3 Distribute 106 books among 8 children. How many books will each child get? How many will be left?

Each child will get _______ books and _______ books will be left.

4 A tailor has 85 buttons. He needs to put 5 buttons on each shirt. On how many shirts can he put these buttons?

He can put these buttons on _____ shirts.

Worksheet

1 Fill each table with the numbers coming out of each division machine. One has been done for each table.

IN → ÷3 → OUT

IN	36	57	132	303	900
OUT	12				

IN → ÷5 → OUT

IN	65	105	405	700	550
OUT			81		

2 Mr Sanjeev sells all types of tyres. Read and answer these questions.

a. There are 48 bicycle tyres. In how many bicycles can we fit these tyres?

b. There are 72 car tyres. In how many cars can we fit these tyres?

c. Buses have six wheels and Mr Sanjeev has 85 bus tyres. In how many buses can we fit these tyres? How many tyres will be left over?

d. Mr Sanjeev stacks lorry tyres in piles of 8 tyres. How many full piles can he make with 45 tyres and how many tyres will be leftover?

_________ piles

_________ leftover tyres

For the Curious Mind

32 balls are put into bags each holding three balls. How many full bags will there be and how many balls are left over?

______ full bags

______ left over

Introduction to Fractions

7

Fraction as Part of a Whole

There are two chocolates. Each of them is cut into two pieces.

Here, both the parts are of the same size.

Here, the parts are not of the same size.

If we cut the chocolate through the middle into two equal parts, then each equal part is called a **half**.

Half is a fraction. Mathematically, it is written as $\frac{1}{2}$.

Remember

Plural of the word 'half' is 'halves'.

One-half

Any object cut into two equal parts is said to be cut into two equal halves. So, one-half is one of the two equal parts.

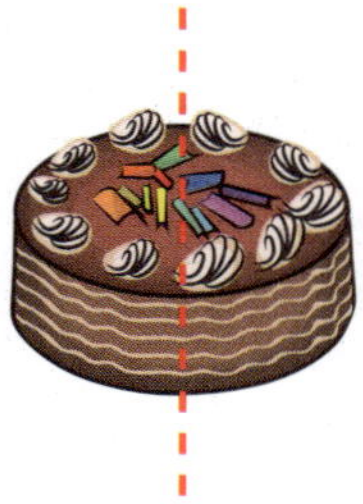

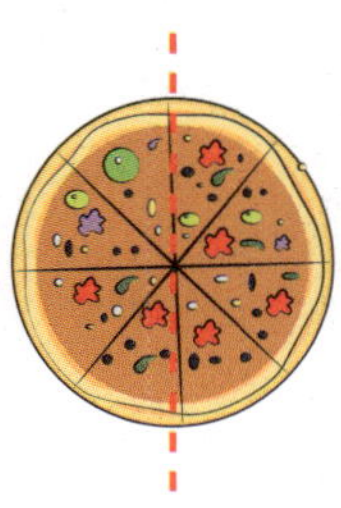

= half of the cake

= $\frac{1}{2}$ cake

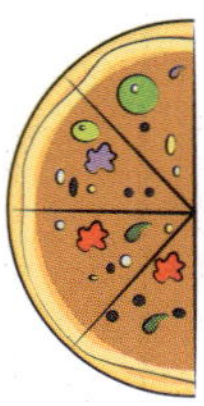

= half of the pizza

= $\frac{1}{2}$ pizza

Examples of one-half

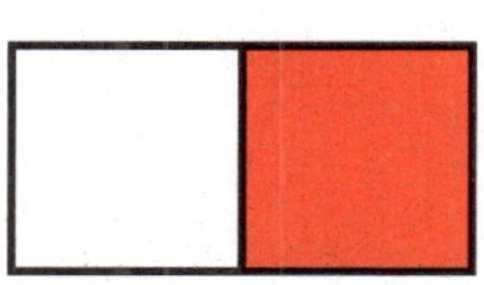

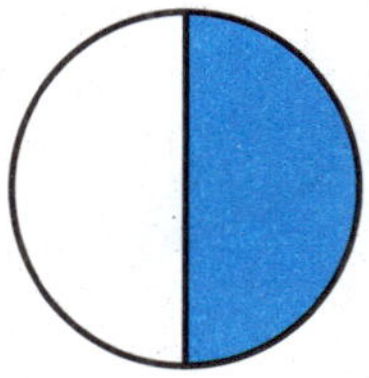

A fraction is a part of a whole object or a collection of objects.

One-third

Just like one-half is one part of two equal parts, one-third is one part of three equal parts.

If we cut a chocolate bar into three equal pieces, then each piece is call **one-third**.

One-third is a fraction. It is written as $\frac{1}{3}$.

More examples of one-third

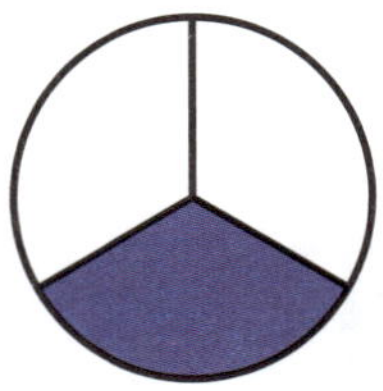

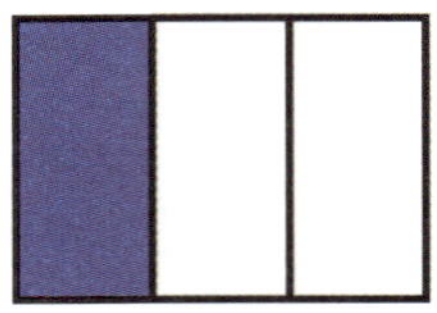

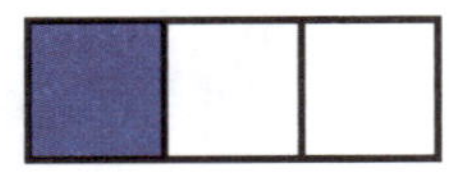

One-fourth

One-fourth is one part of four equal parts.

If we cut a cake into four equal parts, then each part is called **one-fourth**.

One fourth is written as $\frac{1}{4}$.

Note

One fourth is also called a quarter.

One fourth = $\frac{1}{4}$

A quarter = $\frac{1}{4}$

More examples of one-fourth

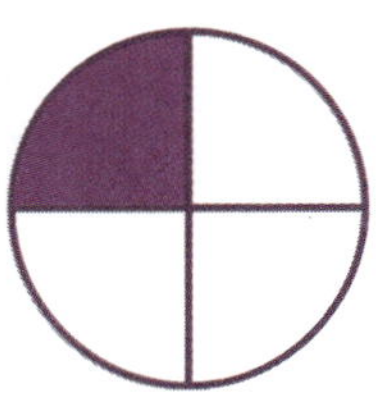

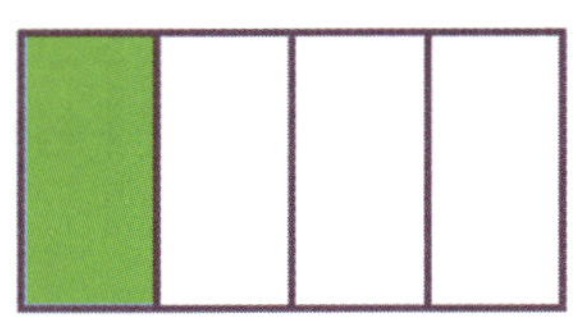

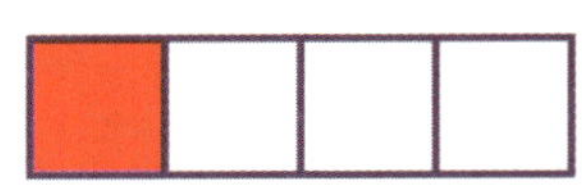

Exercise 7.1

1. **Write the fraction for the shaded portion in each figure.**

a. 

______

b. 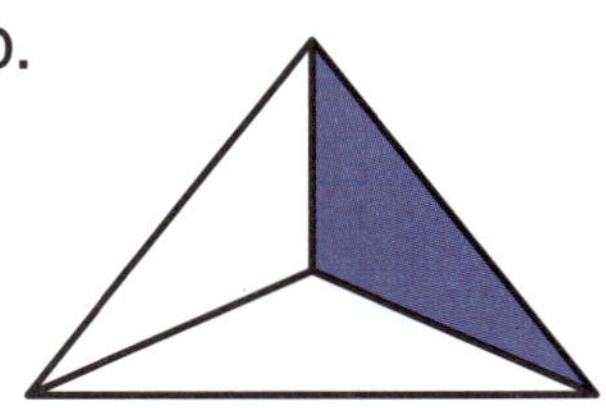

______

c. 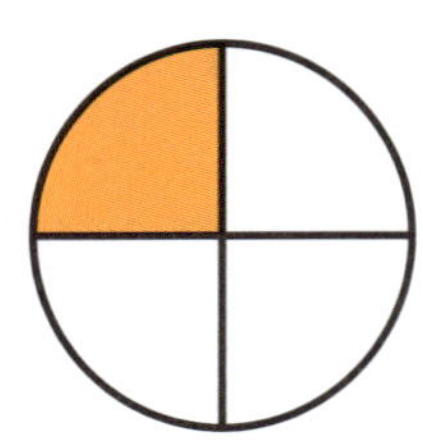

______

2 **Write the fraction for the unshaded portion in each figure.**

a. 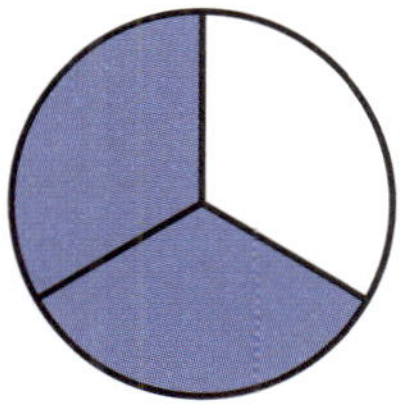

______

b. 

______

Fraction as Part of a Collection

There are two balloons. One balloon is blue. Thus, $\frac{1}{2}$ of the balloons are blue.

This is a group of four pencils. One pencil is green.

Thus, $\frac{1}{4}$ of the pencils are green.

There are three apples. One apple is red.

Thus, $\frac{1}{3}$ of the apples are red.

Exercise 7.2

1 **Colour $\frac{1}{2}$ of the butterflies.**

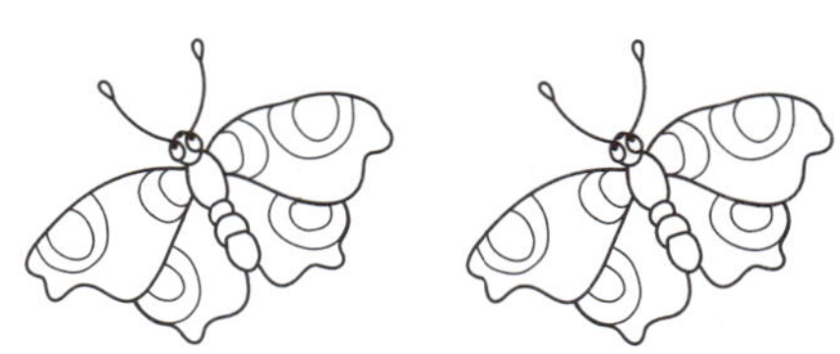

2 **Colour $\frac{1}{3}$ of the carrots.**

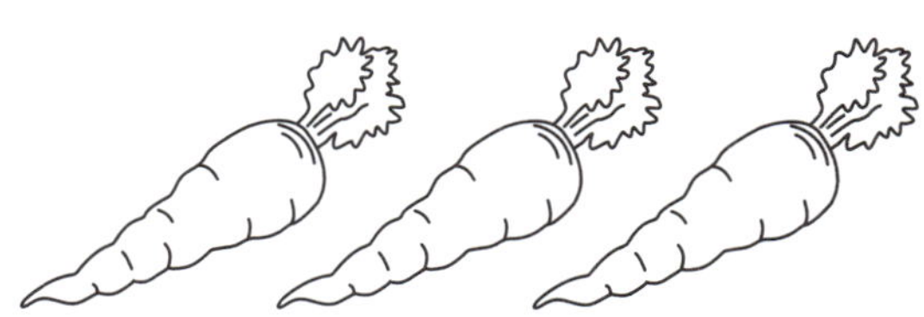

3 **Colour $\frac{1}{4}$ of the tomatoes.**

Revision Exercise

1 **Match the figures in column A to how much they represent in column B. The fractions represent the shaded portion in each figure.**

	A		B
i.		a.	$\frac{1}{2}$
ii.	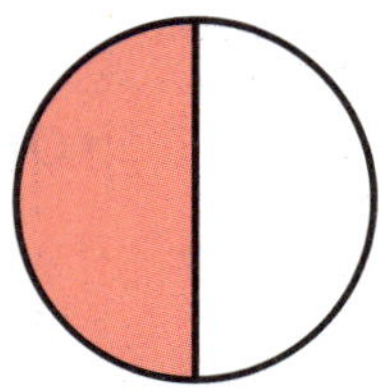	b.	$\frac{1}{3}$
iii.	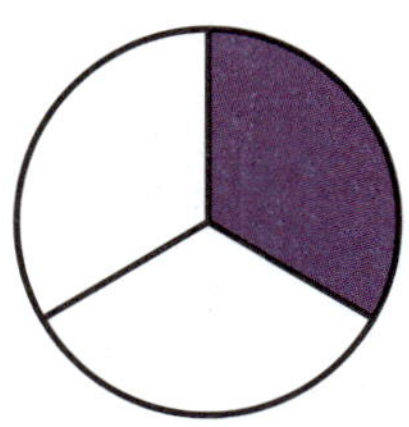	c.	$\frac{1}{4}$

2 **a. Colour $\frac{1}{4}$ of each picture.**

a. 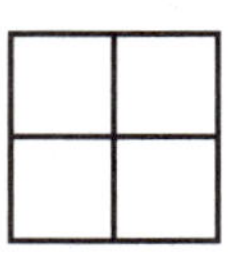
b. 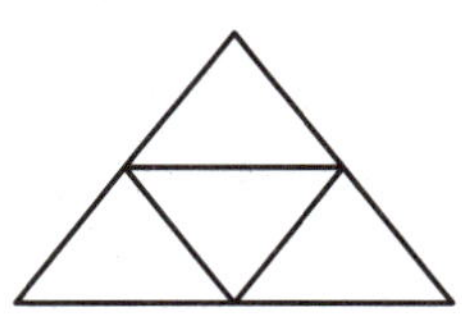
c. 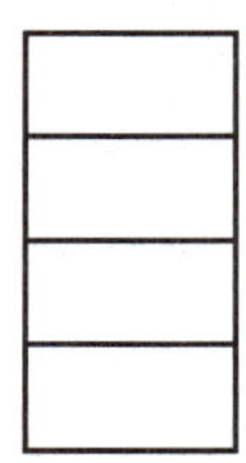
d. 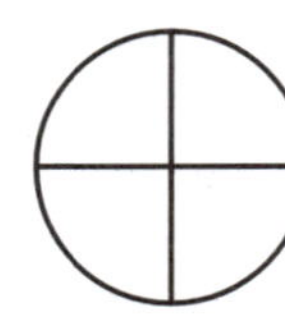

b. Colour $\frac{1}{3}$ of each picture.

a. 
b. 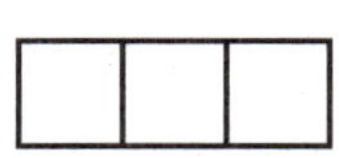
c. 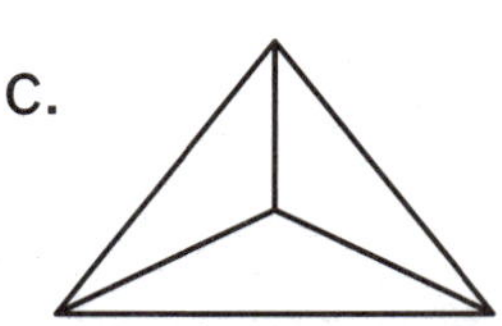
d. 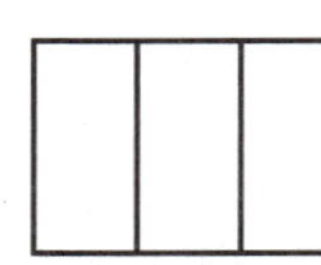

c. Colour $\frac{1}{2}$ of each picture.

a. 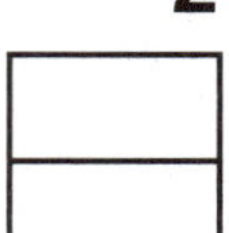
b. 
c. 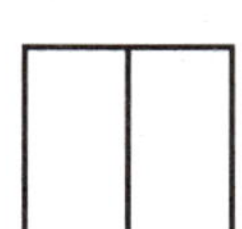
d. 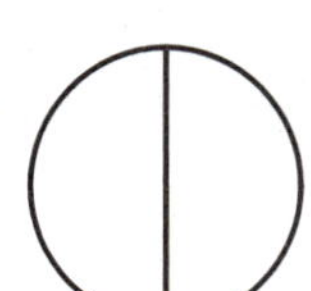
e. 

Mixed Review 2

1. If $7 \times 5 = 35$,

then $35 \div 7 =$ ______ and $35 \div 5 =$ ______.

2. Use long division and short division methods to solve the following.

a. $18 \div 2$

Long division

$2 \overline{)18}$

−
______

______

Quotient: ______

Short division

$2 \underline{|\ 18}$

Quotient: ______

b. $21 \div 3$

Long division

$3 \overline{)21}$

−
______

______

Quotient: ______

Short division

$3 \underline{|\ 21}$

Quotient: ______

c. $32 \div 4$

Long division

$4 \overline{)32}$

−
______

______

Quotient: ______

Short division

$4 \underline{|\ 32}$

Quotient: ______

d. $20 \div 5$

Long division

$5 \overline{)20}$

−
______

______

Quotient: ______

Short division

$5 \underline{|\ 20}$

Quotient: ______

3 **Divide the following using the long division method.**

a. $225 \div 5$

$5\overline{)225}$ Quotient = ______

Remainder = ______

b. $330 \div 3$

$3\overline{)330}$ Quotient = ______

Remainder = ______

c. $104 \div 2$

$2\overline{)104}$ Quotient = ______

Remainder = ______

d. $600 \div 6$

$6\overline{)600}$ Quotient = ______

Remainder = ______

4 **Distribute 126 marbles among 9 girls. How many marbles will each girl get?**

Each girl will get ______ marbles.

5 **Distribute 106 pineapples equally among 8 children. How many pineapples will each child get? How many pineapples will be left?**

Each child will get ______ pineapples. ______ pineapples will be left.

6 **Colour $\frac{1}{3}$ of each picture.**

a. 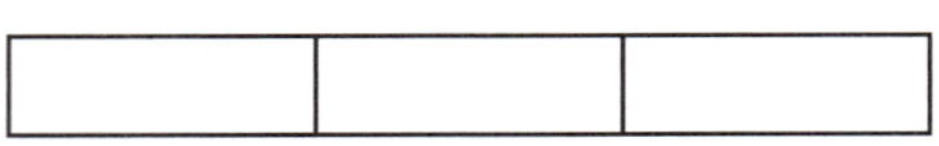

b. 

c. 

7 **Colour $\frac{1}{2}$ of each picture.**

a. 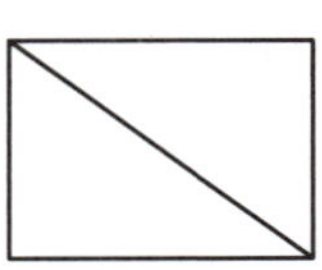

b. 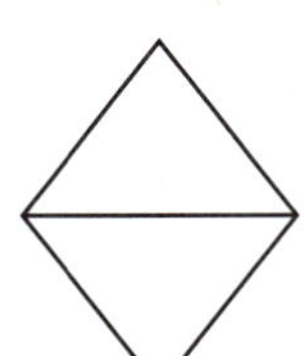

c. 

Measurements

8

Measurements Around Us

In our day-to-day life, we see many people dealing with measurements. Let us look at some examples.

The carpenter measuring the length of the table he is making

The vegetable vendor measuring the weight of the vegetable he is selling

The milkman measuring the amount of the milk he is selling

Measuring Length

We use our handspan, foot span, cubit to get an idea of the length of an object.

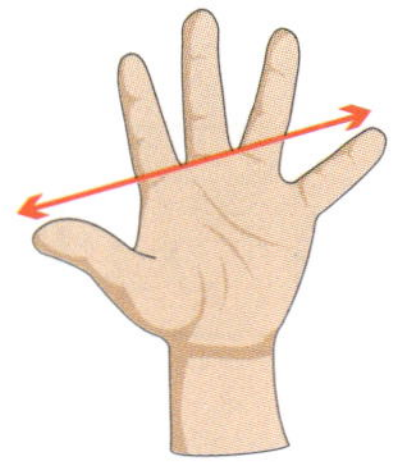

Handspan

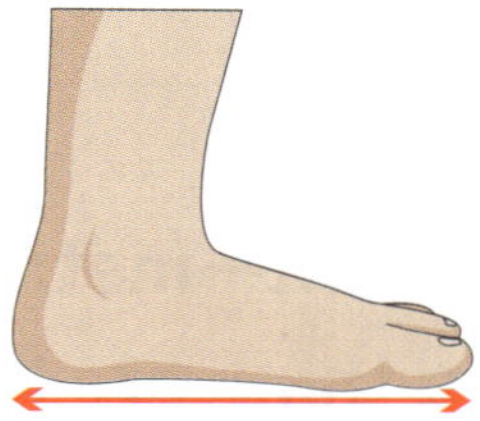

Foot span

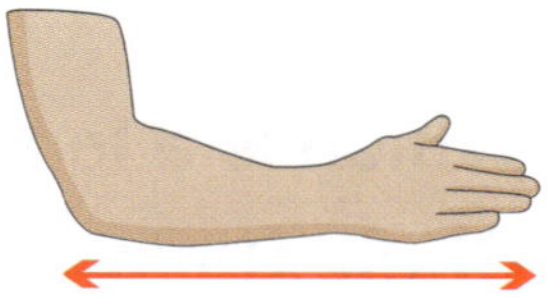

Cubit

Rajiv and Rajiv's father decide to use their handspan to measure a table. Rajiv says that the length of the table is equal to 9 handspans.

But, Rajiv's father says that the length of the table is equal to 6 handspans.

They both got different measurements for the same table because their handspans are different.

To make sure that everyone gets the same measurement, we use standard units of measurements. To measure length, we use fixed measurements called 'metre' and 'centimetre'.

We have fixed tools to measure the length of any object like a ruler.

A centimetre is used to measure short lengths. A centimetre is written as *cm*. Look at a ruler to see the length of a centimetre.

This length is equal to 1 cm.

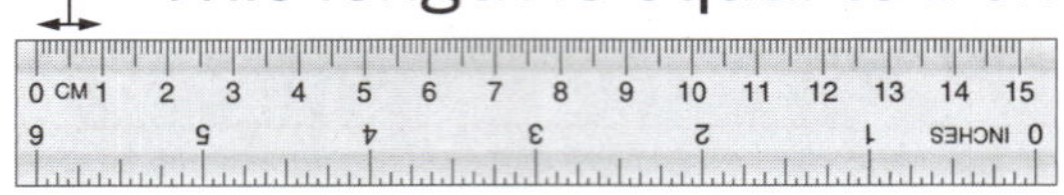

Use your ruler to measure the length of your

a. **Pencil**

Length of the pencil is _______ cm.

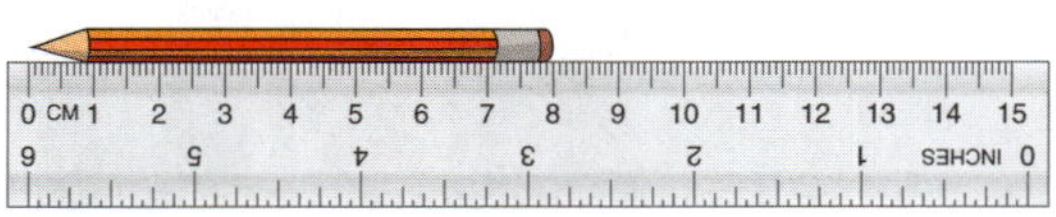

b. **Eraser**

Length of the eraser = _______ cm

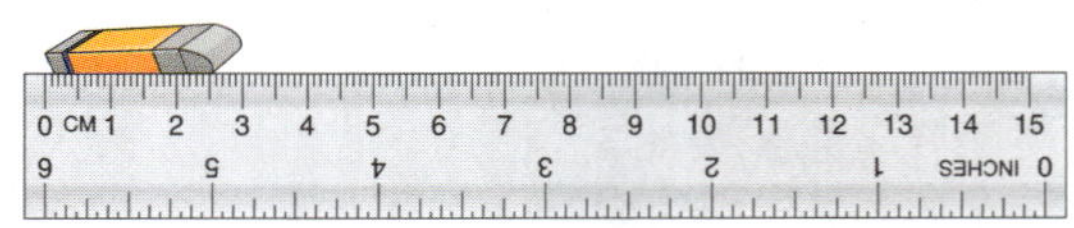

A metre is used to measure longer lengths. A metre is approximately equal to the distance, as shown, between both your hands if you stretch them.

A metre is written as '**m**' in short.

When you go to buy a piece of cloth, the shopkeeper will measure it in metres.

Approximately 1 metre

Remember

1 m = 100 cm

Exercise 8.1

1. **Which is a longer measurement—metre or centimetre? _______**
2. **Circle the pictures that you think are less than 1 metre.**

Length of a bus

Height of a cup

Length of a book

Length of a pencil

Height of a door

Height of a zebra

3 Circle the pictures that you think are more than 1 centimetre.

A dot

Length of a pencil

Length of an ant

Length of a TV

Length of an eraser

4 Write which measurement to use, m or cm, to measure the following.

a. The length of a pencil ______

b. The length of a bed ______

c. The length of an envelope ______

d. The length of a book ______

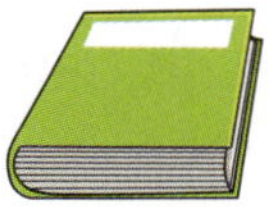

e. The length of a sofa ______

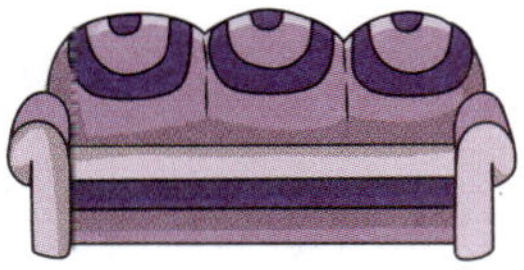

f. The length of a room ______

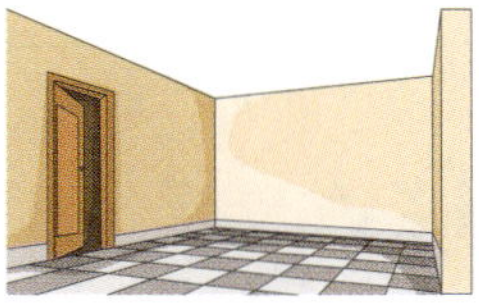

5 Use your ruler to measure the following.

a. The height of a glass = ______ cm

b. The length of a pencil box = ______ cm

c. The height of a candle = ______ cm

Drawing and Measuring Line Segments

To Draw a Line Segment with a Ruler

Draw a line segment 2 cm long with a ruler.

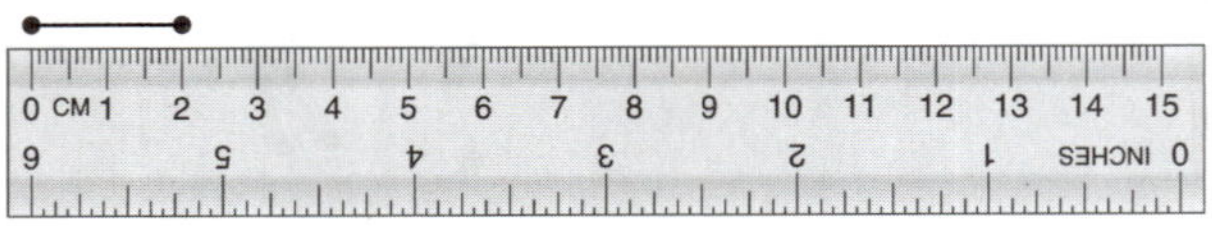

Place the ruler where the line segment is to be drawn.

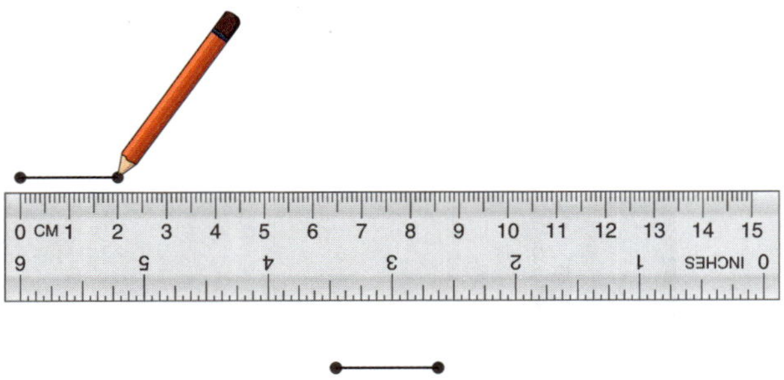

Start drawing the line segment from point 0 to the point 2 along the ruler.

Remove the ruler and the pencil and you will get a line segment 2 cm long.

To Measure the Length of a Line Segment

When a line segment is given and we have to measure its length, place the ruler against the line segment with one end of the line segment at mark 0.

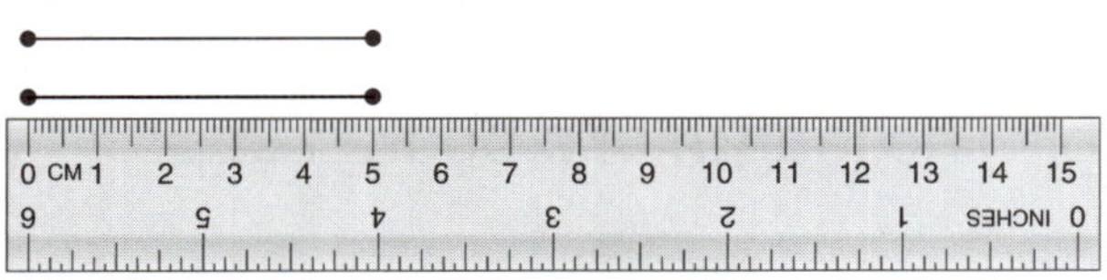

Note the point at which the other end of the line segment ends.

If the line segment ends at 5 cm on the ruler, then the length of the line segment is 5 cm.

Remember

To convert a measurement that is in metres into centimetres, multiply it by 100.

$10 \times 100 = 1000$

$10 \text{ m} = 10 \times 100 = 1000 \text{ cm}$

Try These!

Convert the measurements as required.

3 m = ________ cm

9 m = ________ cm

800 cm = ________ m

700 cm = ________ m

Conversions

Conversion of Metres into Centimetres

Shelly bought 2 m cloth to make a dress. How many centimetres is that?

Length of the cloth = 2 m

2 m = 1 m + 1 m

1 m = 100 cm

Therefore, $2 \text{ m} = 100 \text{ cm} + 100 \text{ cm} = 2 \times 100 \text{ cm} = 200 \text{ cm}$

Conversion of Centimetre to Metre

Karan bought 500 cm string to tie the balloons for a birthday party. How many metres did he buy?

Length of the string = 500 cm

$500 \text{ cm} = 5 \times 100 \text{ cm}$

100 cm = 1 m

Therefore, $500 \text{ cm} = 5 \times 100 \text{ cm} = 5 \times 1 \text{ m} = 5 \text{ m}$

Exercise 8.2

1. **Draw a line segment for each of the lengths given below.**

   a. 2 cm b. 3 cm c. 5 cm

   d. 6 cm e. 7 cm f. 9 cm

2. **Measure the lengths of the following line segments.**

   a.  b.

   c.    d. 

3. **Choose the correct answers from the box and fill in the blanks.**

300	600	900	700

   a. 7 m = ________ cm b. 3 m = ________ cm

   c. 6 m = ________ cm d. 9 m = ________ cm

4. **Convert the following measurements in centimetres into metres.**

   a. 800 cm = ______ m

   b. 400 cm = ______ m

   c. 700 cm = ______ m

   d. 1000 cm = ______ m

Addition and Subtraction of Length

Addition

Example 1: Add 45 cm and 12 cm.

$$\begin{array}{rr} & 45\text{ cm} \\ + & 12\text{ cm} \\ \hline & 57\text{ cm} \\ \hline \end{array}$$

Thus, 45 cm + 12 cm = 57 cm

Note

We add like normal addition, carrying forward wherever required.

Example 2: Add 25 m 73 cm and 8 m 56 cm.

$$\begin{array}{rrr} & \textbf{m} & \textbf{cm} \\ & {}^{1}2\,{}^{1}5 & 73 \\ + & 8 & 56 \\ \hline & 34 & 29 \\ \hline \end{array}$$

Therefore, 25 m 73 cm + 8 m 56 cm = 34 m 29 cm

Example 3: Suresh bought two pieces of cloth for making curtains. One cloth measures 13 m 25 cm and the second cloth measures 2 m 6 cm. What was the total length of the two pieces of cloth?

Length of one cloth = 13 m 25 cm

Length of second cloth = 2 m 6 cm

Total length of the cloth = 13 m 25 cm + 2 m 6 cm

$$\begin{array}{rrr} & \textbf{m} & \textbf{cm} \\ & 13 & {}^{1}25 \\ + & 2 & 06 \\ \hline & 15 & 31 \\ \hline \end{array}$$

Thus, the total length of the two pieces of cloth that Suresh bought was 15 m 31 cm.

Hints and Tips

Since 1 m = 100 cm and 100 has 2 zeros, the cm column should have 2 digits. When a number is expressed in cm with only 1 digit, like 6 cm, then we write it as 06 to make it two digits.

Subtraction

Example 4: 36 m 23 cm – 17 m 48 cm

$$\begin{array}{rrr} & \textbf{m} & \textbf{cm} \\ & {}^{2}\not{3}\,{}^{15}\not{6} & {}^{11}\not{2}\,{}^{13}\not{3} \\ - & 1\;7 & 4\;8 \\ \hline & 1\;8 & 7\;5 \\ \hline \end{array}$$

Note

We subtract like normal subtraction, borrowing wherever required.

Therefore, 36 m 23 cm – 17 m 48 cm = 18 m 75 cm

Example 5: 47 m 82 cm – 19 m 6 cm

$$\begin{array}{rrr} & \textbf{m} & \textbf{cm} \\ & {}^{3}\not{4}\,{}^{17}\not{7} & {}^{7}\not{8}\,{}^{12}\not{2} \\ - & 1\;9 & 0\;6 \\ \hline & 2\;8 & 7\;6 \\ \hline \end{array}$$

Therefore, 47 m 82 cm – 19 m 6 cm = 28 m 76 cm

Mental Maths

Think and answer.

1. 1 m + 100 cm = ___ m
2. 8 m + 100 cm = ___ cm
3. 10 m – 200 cm = ___ m
4. 12 m 12 cm + 11 m 11 cm = ___
5. 50 m 25 cm – 25 m 25 cm = ___

Example 6: Veena bought 15 m cloth from the market to make curtains. She used only 4 m 12 cm. How much cloth was left?

Total cloth bought = 15 m

Cloth used = 4 m 12 cm

Cloth left = 15 m – 4 m 12 cm

$$\begin{array}{rrr} & \textbf{m} & \textbf{cm} \\ & 1\,{}^{4}\not{5} & {}^{9}_{10}\not{0}\,{}^{10}\not{0} \\ - & 4 & 1\;2 \\ \hline & 10 & 8\;8 \\ \hline \end{array}$$

Thus, 10 m 88 cm cloth was left.

Note

When the cm is missing, we write 00.

Exercise 8.3

1 Solve the following.

a.

	m	cm
	15	35
+	63	24

b.

	m	cm
	26	35
+	42	67

c.

	m	cm
	38	49
+	25	72

d.

	m	cm
	46	00
+	18	25

e.

	m	cm
	23	46
+	75	21

f.

	m	cm
	25	17
+	18	23

2 Solve the following.

a.

	m	cm
	68	49
−	25	17

b.

	m	cm
	64	93
−	21	27

c.

	m	cm
	42	35
−	16	47

d.

	m	cm
	39	00
−	18	62

e.

	m	cm
	25	97
−	14	21

f.

	m	cm
	82	51
−	47	39

Do the following sums in your notebook.

3 Solve the following.

a. 35 m 74 cm + 26 m 39 cm

b. 14 m 36 cm + 8 m 3 cm

4 Solve the following.

a. 96 m 24 cm – 18 m 17 cm

b. 35 m 47 cm – 29 m 5 cm

5 Rama bought 2 m 15 cm cloth for a shirt and 2 m 30 cm cloth for a trouser. Find the total cloth that she bought.

Thus,Rama bought ________cloth.

6. Out of 7 m 65 cm of a wall, 3 m 85 cm was painted. How much wall was left to be painted?

Thus, ________ wall was left to be painted.

7. Suman has 3 m cloth. She uses 1 m 20 cm cloth to make a shirt. How much cloth is left?

Thus, ________ cloth is left.

Measuring Weight

If we hold a pencil in one hand and a pencil box in the other hand, we find that the pencil box is heavier than the pencil.

In the first picture shown here, 2 apples weigh the same as 2 stones.

In the second picture, 2 apples weigh the same as 1 stone.

This is because the stone in the second picture is bigger.

We use standard units of 'kilogram' and 'gram' to weigh objects.

Kilogram is written as '**kg**' in short.

Gram is written as '**g**' in short.

Grams are used to weigh lighter objects.

Note

$\frac{1}{2}$ kilogram = 500 gram

1 kilogram = 1000 gram

A teaspoon of salt weighs about 5 grams.

A tablespoon of salt weighs about 15 grams.

2 big pieces of ginger will weigh about 100 grams.

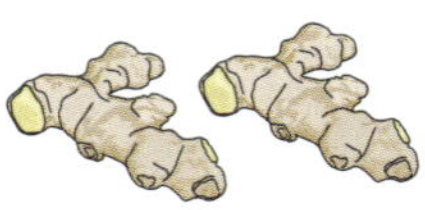

5 big pieces of ginger will weigh about 250 grams.

3 apples will weigh about 500 gram or $\frac{1}{2}$ kilogram.

6 apples will weigh about 1 kilogram.

Note

Heavier objects are weighed in kilograms.

Lighter objects are weighed in grams.

Different types of weighing scales

Relationship between Kilogram and Gram

1 kg = 1000 g

1 becomes 1000. It increases in value numerically. Whenever something increases in value, we multiply. So, to convert kilogram to gram we multiply by 1000.

Conversion of Gram to Kilogram

1000 g = 1 kg

1000 becomes 1, it becomes 'less' numerically, so we divide by 1000.

Note

To convert kg to g, multiply by 1000.
To convert g to kg, divide by 1000.

Exercise 8.4

1. **Tick the weight you think is correct.**

500 g or 500 kg | 2 g or 2 kg | 15 g or 15 kg | 1 g or 1 kg | 10 g or 10 kg

2 **Circle the objects that you think weigh more than 1 kg.**

3 **Write the weights of the given objects.**

a. 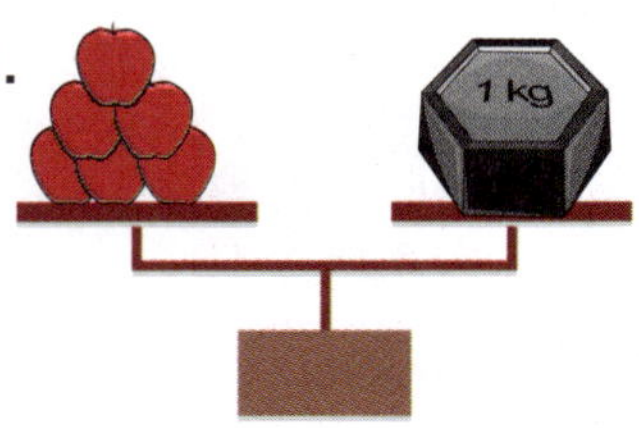

____

b. 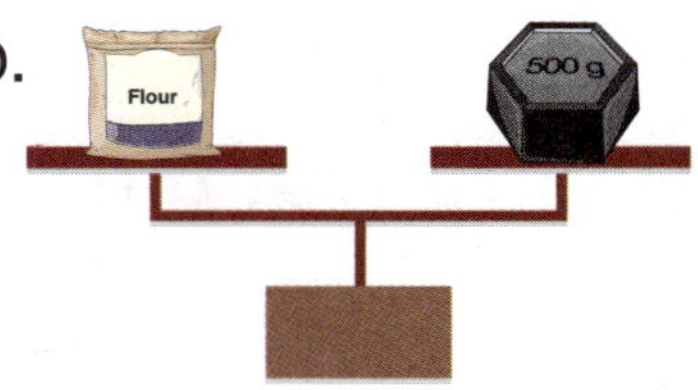

____

c. 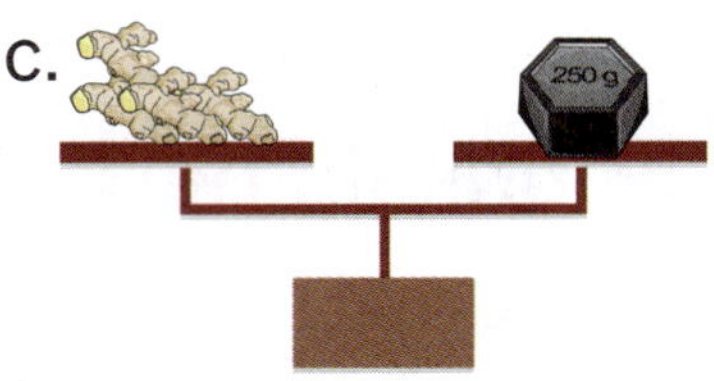

____

d. 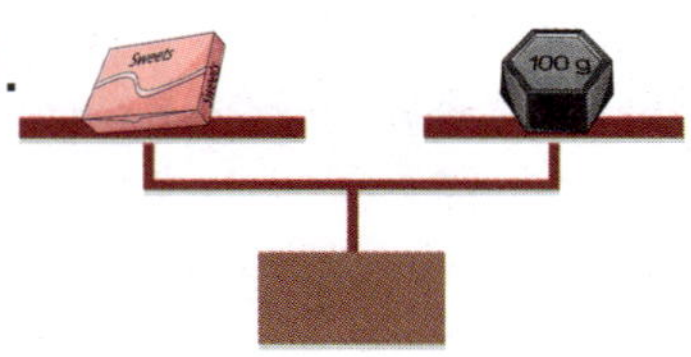

____

e. 

____

f. 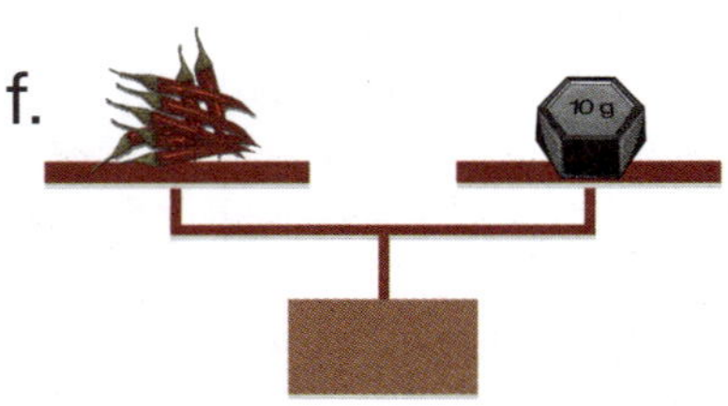

____

Addition and Subtraction of Weight

Addition

kg and g are added in the same way as we add cm and m.

Example 1: Add 13 kg 275 g and 4 kg 182 g.

	kg	g
	13	[1]275
+	4	182
	17	457

Thus, 13 kg 275 g + 4 kg 182 g =17 kg 457 g

Example 2: Add 12 kg 492 g and 5 kg 8 g.

	kg	g
	12	[1]4 [1]92
+	5	008
	17	500

Note

Since 1 kg = 1000 g, we should have 3 digits in g. So, 8 g is written as 008 g.

Thus, 12 kg 492 g + 5 kg 8 g = 17 Kg 500 g

Subtraction

Example 3: 42 kg 361 g – 17 kg 4 g

	kg	g
	[3]~~4~~ [12]~~2~~	3 [5]~~6~~ [11]~~1~~
–	1 7	0 0 4
	2 5	3 5 7

Thus, 42 kg 361 g – 17 kg 4 g = 25 kg 357 g

Example 4: 52 kg – 3 kg 178 g

	kg	g
	[4]~~5~~ [11 / 1]~~2~~	[9 / 10]~~0~~ [9 / 10]~~0~~ [10]~~0~~
–	3	1 7 8
	4 8	8 2 2

Note

Where there is no 'g' given, we have to write 000 in place of 'g' as 1 kg = 1000 'g'.

Thus, 52 kg – 3 kg 178 g = 48 kg 822 g

Example 5: Susan bought 1 kg 250 g of potatoes and 2 kg 125 g of onions. What is the total weight of the vegetables that Susan bought?

Amount of potatoes = 1 kg 250 g

Amount of onions = 2 kg 125 g

Total weight of the vegetables = 1 kg 250 g+ 2 kg 125 g

	kg	g
Potatoes =	1	250
Onions =	+2	125
	3	375

Thus, Susan bought 3 kg 375 g of vegetables.

Exercise 8.5

1 Solve the following.

a.

	kg	g
	12	342
+	35	216

b.

	kg	g
	47	519
+	15	328

c.

	kg	g
	29	675
+	13	248

d.
	kg	g
	35	000
+	18	764

e.
	kg	g
	63	572
+		186

f.
	kg	g
	49	348
+	26	000

2 **Solve the following.**

a.
	kg	g
	8	976
–	5	213

b.
	kg	g
	7	235
–	1	649

c.
	kg	g
	12	720
–	9	160

d.
	kg	g
	39	259
–	18	000

e.
	kg	g
	45	000
–	29	347

f.
	kg	g
	16	234
–		789

3 **Solve the following.**

a. 15 kg 365 g + 27 kg 172 g

b. 47 kg 180 g + 9 kg 5 g

c. 8 kg 12 g + 7 kg 16 g

d. 32 kg + 5 kg 189 g

4 **Solve the following.**

a. 82 kg 765 g – 41 kg 612 g

b. 49 kg 234 g – 18 kg 756 g

c. 32 kg 180 g – 5 kg 7 g

d. 67 kg 23 g – 18 kg 46 g

5 A bicycle weighs 10 kg 250 g. Reena weighs 25 kg 175 g. What is the total weight of the bicycle and Reena?

Thus, the total weight of the bicycle and Reena is ______________.

6 Gautam's weight is 29 kg 750 g and Jatin's weight is 18 kg 990 g. Who weighs more and by how much?

Thus, _________ weighs more by ____________.

7. A school bag with books weighs 4 kg 370 g. If the books weigh 3 kg 750 g, what is the weight of the bag?

Thus, the weight of the bag is ______.

Measuring Capacity

Capacity of a container is equal to the amount of liquid that it can hold.

We use the standard measurements 'litres' and 'millilitres' to measure capacity. Litres is written as 'ℓ' and millilitres is written as '**mℓ**'

The unit **millilitre** is used to measure smaller quantities of liquid. The unit **litre** is used to measure larger quantities of liquid.

1 teaspoon of liquid medicine is about 5 mℓ.

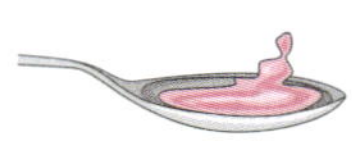

5 mℓ

1 tablespoon of liquid medicine is about 15 mℓ.

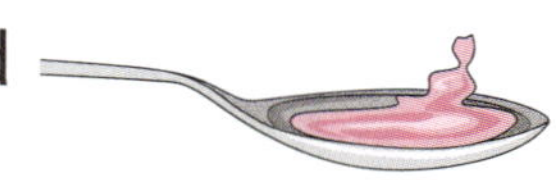

15 mℓ

A glass of water is about 200 mℓ.

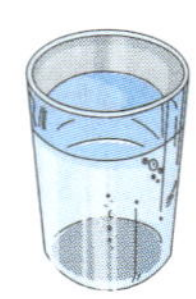

200 mℓ

A bottle of soft drink is about 1 ℓ.

1 ℓ

A bucket of water is about 15 ℓ.

15 ℓ

Relationship between Litres and Millilitres

1 ℓ = 1000 mℓ. '1' becomes '1000'. It becomes 'more' numerically. So, we multiply by 1000.

Example 1: Convert 2 ℓ to mℓ.

2 ℓ = 2 × 1000 = 2000 mℓ

Example 2: Convert 5 ℓ 260 mℓ to mℓ.

5 ℓ = 5 × 1000 = 5000 mℓ

260 mℓ = + 260 mℓ

5260

5 ℓ 260 mℓ = 5260 mℓ

Conversion of Millilitres to Litres

1000 mℓ = 1 ℓ. '1000' becomes '1'. It becomes 'less' numerically. So, we divide by 1000.

Example 3: Convert 6000 mℓ to ℓ and mℓ.

6000 mℓ = 6000 ÷ 1000
= 6 ℓ

Example 4: Convert 3645 mℓ to ℓ and mℓ.

3645 mℓ = 36450 ÷ 1000
= 3 ℓ 645 mℓ

Exercise 8.6

1. **Tick the measurement you think is correct.**

 5 mℓ or 5 ℓ

 15 mℓ or 15 ℓ

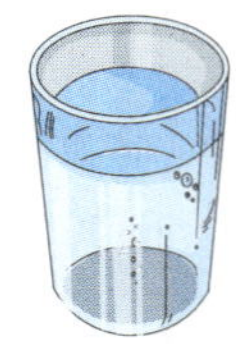 200 mℓ or 200 ℓ

 750 mℓ or 750 ℓ

 1 mℓ or 1 ℓ

 250 mℓ or 250 ℓ

2. **Tick the objects that you think should be measured in litres and cross the ones you think should be measured in millilitres.**

 ☐

 ☐

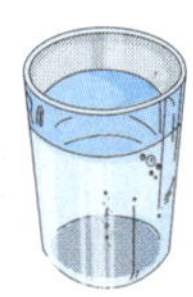 ☐

 ☐

 ☐

 ☐

☐

☐

 ☐

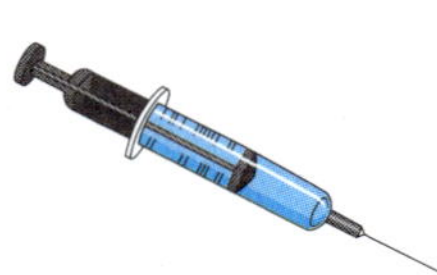 ☐

 ☐

 ☐

Addition and Subtraction of Capacity

Addition

Example 1:

Add 12 ℓ 350 mℓ and 5 ℓ 173 mℓ.

	ℓ	mℓ
	12	[1]350
+	5	173
	17	523

Thus, 12 ℓ 350 mℓ + 5 ℓ 173 mℓ = 17 ℓ 523 mℓ

Example 2:

Add 15 ℓ 794 mℓ and 8 ℓ 6 mℓ.

	ℓ	mℓ
	[1]15	[1]7[1]94
+	8	006
	23	800

Thus, 15 ℓ 794 mℓ + 8 ℓ 6 mℓ = 23 ℓ 800 mℓ

Note

Since 1 ℓ = 1000 mℓ, we should have 3 digits in mℓ.

So, 6 mℓ is written as 006 mℓ.

Subtraction

Example 3:

53 ℓ 492 mℓ – 28 ℓ 576 mℓ

	ℓ	mℓ
	4 12	14 8 12
	~~5~~ ~~3~~	~~4~~ ~~9~~ ~~2~~
–	2 8	5 7 6
	2 4	9 1 6

Thus, 53 ℓ 492 mℓ – 28 576 mℓ = 24 ℓ 916 mℓ

Example 4:

28 ℓ 345 mℓ – 13 ℓ 9 mℓ

	ℓ	mℓ
		3 15
	28	3 ~~4~~ ~~5~~
–	13	0 0 9
	15	3 3 6

Thus, 28 ℓ 345 mℓ – 13 ℓ 9 mℓ = 15 ℓ 336 mℓ

Example 5:

19 ℓ – 5 ℓ 263 mℓ

	ℓ	mℓ
	8	9 9
		10 10 10
	1 ~~9~~	~~0~~ ~~0~~ ~~0~~
–	0 5	2 6 3
	1 3	7 3 7

Thus, 19 ℓ – 5 ℓ 263 mℓ = 13 ℓ 737 mℓ

Exercise 8.7

1 Solve the following.

a.

	ℓ	mℓ
	13	425
+	72	163

b.

	ℓ	mℓ
	35	268
+	18	724

c.

	ℓ	mℓ
	42	000
+	34	296

d.

	ℓ	mℓ
	51	792
+		235

e.

	ℓ	mℓ
	73	254
+	19	000

f.

	ℓ	mℓ
	12	569
+	8	001

2 **Solve the following.**

a.

ℓ	mℓ
9	876
− 4	312

b.

ℓ	mℓ
8	265
− 2	197

c.

ℓ	mℓ
25	350
− 8	170

d.

ℓ	mℓ
42	295
− 11	000

e.

ℓ	mℓ
62	000
− 49	183

f.

ℓ	mℓ
15	382
−	967

3 **Solve the following.**

a. 14 ℓ 863 mℓ + 32 ℓ 159 mℓ

b. 27 ℓ 583 mℓ + 4 ℓ 7 mℓ

c. 2 ℓ 13 mℓ + 5 ℓ 18 mℓ

d. 16 ℓ + 1 ℓ 230 mℓ

4 **Solve the following.**

a. 49 ℓ 875 mℓ − 18 ℓ 624 mℓ

b. 63 ℓ 240 mℓ − 29 ℓ 756 mℓ

c. 28 ℓ 394 mℓ − 9 ℓ 5 mℓ

d. 35 ℓ 28 mℓ − 17 ℓ 49 mℓ

5 Rohit used 25 ℓ 750 mℓ of water to water the garden and 5 ℓ 250 mℓ of water to wash his car. What was the total amount of water that Rohit used?

Thus, Rohit used ______water.

6 A bucket had 14 ℓ 250 mℓ of water in it. Rani used 5 ℓ 375 mℓ. How much water was left in the bucket?

Thus, ________water was left in the bucket.

7 Reena drank 200 mℓ of juice and Sunita drank 1 ℓ 150 mℓ of juice. How much juice did both the girls drink?

Thus, both the girls drank ________ of juice.

Revision Exercise

1 Tick the correct length.

a. The length of the bench is about 2 cm/2 m.

b. The length of the cellphone is about 7 cm/7 m.

2 Tick the correct weight.

a. The weight of this apple is about 200 g/200 kg.

b. Mr Gupta's weight is about 70 g/70 kg.

3 Tick the correct capacity.

a. The amount of shampoo in this bottle is about 250 mℓ / 250 ℓ.

b. The amount of oil in this bottle is about 5 mℓ / 5 ℓ.

4 The distance from Anil's house to his school is 5 km 120 m. How much distance does he cover to go to school and come back in one day?

Thus, Amit covers ________distance in one day.

5 A basket of flowers weighs 2 kg 120 g and a box of chocolates weighs 1 kg 795 g. What weighs more and by how much?

Thus, __________weighs more by ________.

6 A bucket holds 15 ℓ of water. A tub holds 20 ℓ 700 mℓ of water. Which one holds more water and by how much?

Thus, ______holds more water by________.

Worksheet

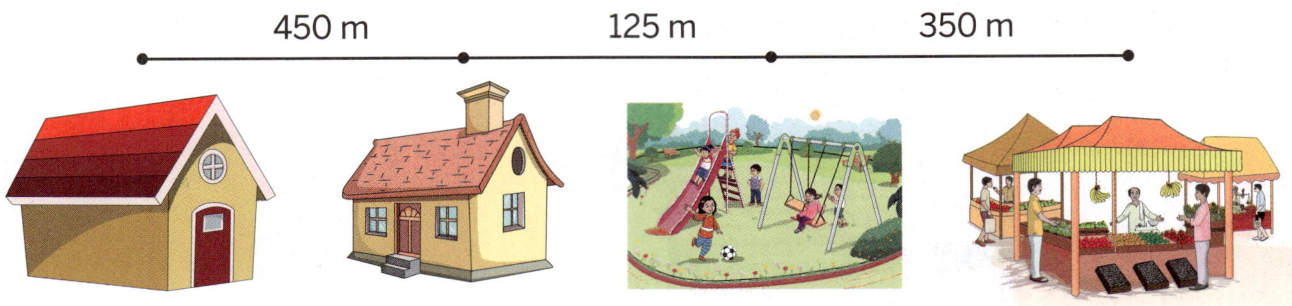

Ajay's house | Vijay's house | Park | Market

1. Ajay walks from his house to Vijay's house. How much distance is that?

2. From Vijay's house, both the boys walk to the park. How much distance is that?

3. Is the park closer to Ajay's house or Vijay's house?

4. What is the total distance that Ajay walks to reach the park?

5. From the park, both the boys walks to the market. How much distance is that?

6. **Tick the longest distance and cross the shortest distance.**

   a. Ajay's house to Vijay's house ☐

   b. Vijay's house to the park ☐

   c. Park to the market ☐

Money

9

Indian Rupee

We use money to buy things from the market. The money used by a country is called its currency. Every country has its own currency which is made of notes and coins. The Indian currency is called Rupees and Paise.

Following are the pictures of Indian currency notes. The value of each note is written on both the sides.

2 rupees

5 rupees

Remember

1 rupee is called *rupee*, while more than 1 rupee is called *rupees*.

10 rupees

20 rupees

50 rupees

100 rupees

500 rupees

1000 rupees

In India, we use the following coins. The value of each coin is written on it on one side.

25 paise

50 paise

1 rupee

2 rupees

5 rupees

10 rupees

Rupees is represented by ₹ or Rs. Paise is represented by p.

Calculating Money

When we go to a shop, we pay the shopkeeper for the things we buy. This often requires us to add or subtract money. Adding or subtracting money is just like adding or subtracting numbers.

Example 1: Find the total amount of money in each case.

a.  +  +  = ₹10 + ₹5 + ₹1 = ₹16

b.  +  + 

= ₹500 + ₹100 + ₹50 = ₹650

Example 2: Compare the amounts and write >, < or =.

 +  +  (>)

 +  + 

Exercise 9.1

1 Find the total amount of money in each case.

a.  +  = ₹ ________

b.  +  +  = ₹ ________

c.  +  = ₹ ________

d.  +  +  = ₹ ________

e.  = ₹ ________

f.  = ₹ ________

2 **Compare the amounts and fill in >, < or =.**

a. 

b. 

c. 

d. 

e. 

Word Problems

Example 1: I bought four gifts for ₹250 and a cake for ₹125. How much money did I spend?

Money spent on gifts		2	5	0
Money spent on cake	+	1	2	5
		3	7	5

Thus, I spent ₹375.

Example 2: A pair of shoes costs ₹995. A pair of socks cost ₹43. How much more do the shoes cost than the socks?

Cost of a pair of shoes = ₹995

Cost of a pair of socks = ₹43

Difference in cost =

$$\begin{array}{rccc} & 9 & 9 & 5 \\ - & & 4 & 3 \\ \hline & 9 & 5 & 2 \end{array}$$

So, the shoes cost ₹952 more.

Example 3: I want to buy a toy for ₹325. If I give the shopkeeper ₹500, how much money will he return?

$$\begin{array}{rccc} & & 9 & \\ & 4 & \cancel{10} & 10 \\ & \cancel{5} & \cancel{0} & \cancel{0} \\ - & 3 & 2 & 5 \\ \hline & 1 & 7 & 5 \\ \hline \end{array}$$

Thus, the shopkeeper will return ₹175.

Example 4: If one pen costs ₹45, how much will seven pens cost?

$$\begin{array}{lccc} \text{One pen costs} & & {}^{3}4 & 5 \\ \text{Seven pens will cost} & & \times & 7 \\ \hline & 3 & 1 & 5 \\ \hline \end{array}$$

Thus, seven pens will cost ₹315.

Example 5: If ₹80 is to be divided equally among 4 people, how much will each person get?

Total money = 80

Number of people = 4

Thus, each person will get ₹20.

$$\begin{array}{r} 20 \\ 4\overline{)80} \\ -8\downarrow \\ \hline 00 \end{array}$$

Exercise 9.2

1. A lamp costs ₹835 and a book costs ₹105. How much do both the things cost?

	H	T	O
Lamp costs			
Book costs			

Thus, both the things cost ₹ ______.

2. Ram has ₹750. Shyam has ₹525. How much more money does Ram have than Shyam?

Ram has ₹ ______.

Shyam has ₹ ______.

Thus, Ram has ₹ ______ more than Shyam.

3. A bag of oranges costs ₹55. How much will seven bags of oranges cost?

A bag costs ₹ ______.

Seven bags will cost ₹ ______.

Thus, 7 bags of oranges will cost ₹ ______.

4. If ₹324 is distributed among 6 people, how much will each person get?

Total money = ₹ ______.

Number of people = ______.

Thus, each person will get ₹ ______.

5. Priyanka collected ₹257 and Samira collected ₹324. How much money did both the girls collect?

Priyanka collected ₹ ______.

Samira collected ₹ ______.

Thus, both the girls collected ₹ ______.

6. I want to buy a pen for ₹64. If I give the shopkeeper ₹100, how much money will he return to me?

Thus, the shopkeeper will return ₹ ______.

7. I want to buy a table for ₹495. If I give the shopkeeper ₹500, how much money will he return to me?

Thus, he will return ₹ ________ to me.

8. A box of chocolates costs ₹60. How much will nine boxes of chocolates cost?

Thus, 9 boxes of chocolates will cost ₹ ________.

9. If ₹343 is to be divided equally among 7 people, how much will each person get?

Thus, each person will get ₹ ________.

10. 5 children collect money for buying a storybook. Each child brings ₹20. What is the total amount they collect?

Thus, 5 children will collect ₹ ________

11. A bag contains 40 marbles. How many marbles will be contained in 9 such bags?

Thus, 9 bags will have ________ marbles.

Revision Exercise

1 **Fill in >, < or =.**

a. 

b. 

c. 

d. 

e. 

2 **Find the total amount of money in each case.**

a.  = ₹ ________

b.  = ₹ ________

c.  = ₹ ________

d.  = ₹ ________

e.  = ₹ ________

f.  = ₹ ________

g.  = ₹ ________

3. I want to buy a dress for ₹925. I have only ₹750 with me. How much more money will I need?

   The cost of the dress is ₹ ________.

   I have ₹ ________.

   I will need ₹ ________.

4. A bouquet of flowers costs ₹350. How much will four such bouquets of flowers cost?

   A bouquet costs ₹ ________.

   Thus, four bouquets will cost ₹ ________.

5. Distribute ₹755 among 5 people. How much will each person get?

   Total money = ₹ ________

   Number of people = ________

   Thus, each person will get ₹ ________.

6. A chair costs ₹650. A lamp costs ₹275. How much do both the things cost?

   A lamp costs ₹ ________.

   A chair costs ₹ ________.

   Thus, both the things will cost ₹ ________.

7. Ramesh bought a book costing ₹575. He gave the shopkeeper ₹600. How much money will the shopkeeper return to Ramesh?

   Cost of the book = ₹ ________

   Amount given to the shopkeeper = ₹ ________

   Balance amount = ₹ ________

Mental Maths

1. If one chocolate costs ₹15, how much does 10 chocolates cost?

2. I want to buy a shirt for ₹125 and a sweater for ₹120. I give the shopkeeper ₹500. How much money will the shopkeeper return?

Worksheet

1 Fill in the missing amounts in the following bills.

Item	Cost per item	Price in ₹
1 bracelet	50	50
2 block sets	110	_____
4 pairs of earrings	12	_____
3 racing cars	_____	60
1 snakes and ladders	_____	100
Total	_____	_____

2 Circle the errors in the bills given below. Write the correct amount and find the total amount to be paid to the shopkeeper. The cost of each item is given correctly.

Item	Cost per item	Price	Correct amount
1 Doll house	350	380	_____
3 soft toys	30	40	_____
3 sets (2 dolls and one doll house)	400	_____	_____
Total	_____	_____	_____

Mental Maths

1. The entry ticket to the New Year Fair for an adult is ₹155 and that for a child is ₹75. How much more is the ticket of an adult than that of a child?

2. If your pocket money per month is ₹25 and you spent ₹20 by the 15th of the month, how much money is left? If you want to buy a pair of painting brushes for ₹100, how much more do you need to buy them?

Time

10

Hours of the Day

A day is divided into different parts. There are 24 hours in a day.

The time between a sunrise and a sunset is called the day. 12 o'clock during the day is called noon. The time after 12 o'clock is called the afternoon time. The time after 5 o'clock is called the evening time. The time between a sunset and a sunrise is called the night.

The clock tells us exactly what time of the day it is.

The long hand is called the minute hand. It takes one full circle in one hour. The short hand is the hour hand. It moves from one number to the next in one hour. One hour = 60 minutes.

In the picture of the clock shown here, the long hand (minute hand) is at 12 and the short hand (hour hand) is at 8. The time is 8 o'clock or 8:00.

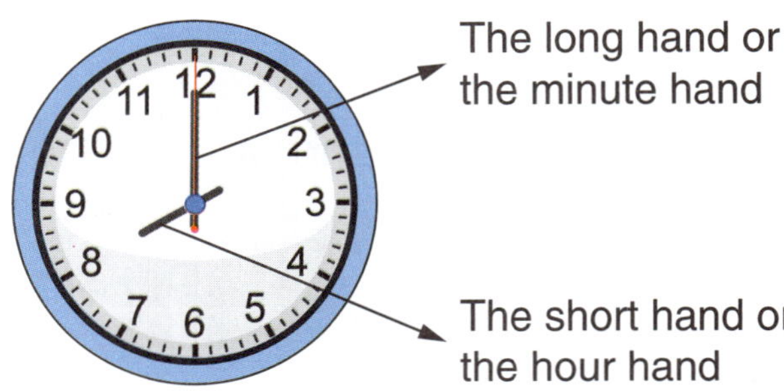

In this picture, the minute hand is at 12 and the hour hand is at 2. The time is 2 o'clock or 2:00.

2 o'clock or 2:00

When both the hands are at 12, the time is 12 o'clock.

Try These!

________ or ________

Exercise 10.1

1. **Write the time shown in the following clocks. One has been done for you.**

1 o'clock ________

or

1:00 ________

____

or

____

____

or

____

____

or

____

2. **Draw the hands to show the time given.**

3 o'clock

or

3:00

5 o'clock

or

5:00

7 o'clock

or

7:00

9 o'clock

or

9:00

Reading Time to Half Past the Hour

The minute hand takes one hour to go around the clock once. During the same time, the hour hand goes from one number to the next number. When the minute hand (long hand) is at 6, we read the time as half past an hour.

When the short hand (hour hand) is between 1 and 2, and the long hand (minute hand) is at 6, the time is 1:30 (one thirty) or half past 1.

Try These!

When the short hand (hour hand) is between 6 and 7, and the long hand (minute hand) is at 6, the time is ________ or ________.

Look at this clock and write the time shown.

________ or ________

When the short hand (hour hand) is between 4 and 5, and the long hand (minute hand) is at 6, the time is 4:30 (four thirty) or half past 4.

When the short hand (hour hand) is between 12 and 1, and the long hand (minute hand) is at 6, the time is 12:30 (twelve thirty) or half past 12.

Reading Time to Quarter Past and Quarter to the Hour

When the short hand (hour hand) is between 12 and 1, and the long hand (minute hand) is at 3, the time is 12:15; read as 'twelve fifteen' or 'quarter past 12'.

When the short hand (hour hand) is between 12 and 1, and the long hand (minute hand) is at 9, the time is 12:45; read as 'twelve forty-five' or 'quarter to 1'.

Exercise 10.2

1 **Write the time shown in the following clocks. One has been done for you.**

11:30
or
Half past 11

____
or
____

____
or
____

____
or
____

____
or
____

____
or
____

____
or
____

____
or
____

2 **Draw the hands for the time given.**

5:30
or
Half past 5

2:15
or
Quarter past 2

1:30
or
Half past 1

7:45
or
Quarter to 8

10:30
or
Half past 10

4:45
or
Quarter to 5

8:15
or
Quarter past 8

3:30
or
Half past 3

Reading Time to 5 Minute Correctness

When the hour hand moves from one number to the next, one hour has passed. In that time, the minute hand has passed 60 minutes. When the minute hand moves from one number to the next, the time taken is 5 minutes. If you know the multiplication table of 5, it is easier to read the time.

5 : 00 or 5 o'clock	5 : 05 or 5 minutes past 5	5 : 10 or 10 minutes past 5	5 : 15 or 15 minutes past 5

Get an Idea about Time

Start playing with your friends at 5 o'clock in the evening and finish playing at 6 o'clock. This will give you an idea about how long an hour is.

Watch the long hand (minute hand) move from 3 to 4. That will show you how long 5 minutes are.

Days of the Week

1 week has 7 days. They are:

Monday Tuesday Wednesday Thursday Friday Saturday Sunday

Monday is the first day of the week.

Saturday and **Sunday** make the weekend.

Sunday is a holiday in most of the countries.

Yesterday, Today and Tomorrow

If today is Wednesday, then yesterday was the day before today, that is, Tuesday. Tomorrow is the day after today, that is, Thursday.

Yesterday	Today	Tomorrow
↓	↓	↓
Tuesday	Wednesday	Thursday

Exercise 10.3

1. Learn the days of the week and fill in the blanks.
   a. A week has ________ days.
   b. ________ comes before Tuesday.
   c. Friday comes after ________.
   d. ________ comes after Tuesday.
2. If today is Tuesday, then
   yesterday was ________. tomorrow will be ________.
3. If today is Friday, then
   yesterday was ________. tomorrow will be ________.
4. If today is Sunday, then
   yesterday was ________. tomorrow will be ________.
5. If today is Wednesday, then
   yesterday was ________. tomorrow will be ________.
6. If today is Saturday, then
   yesterday was ________. tomorrow will be ________.

Months of the Year

A year has 12 months. Their names are given below with the number of days in each month.

Months	Written as	Number of days
January	Jan	31
February	Feb	28 or 29
March	Mar	31
April	Apr	30
May	May	31
June	June	30
July	July	31
August	Aug	31
September	Sep	30
October	Oct	31
November	Nov	30
December	Dec	31

Note

February normally has 28 days but once every 4 years, it has 29 days.

Some Points to Remember

1. Months have 30 or 31 days alternately.
2. February is the only month which has 28 or 29 days.
3. July, August and December, January are the only two pairs of consecutive months which have 31 days.

You can remember the number of days in each month with the help of your fist.

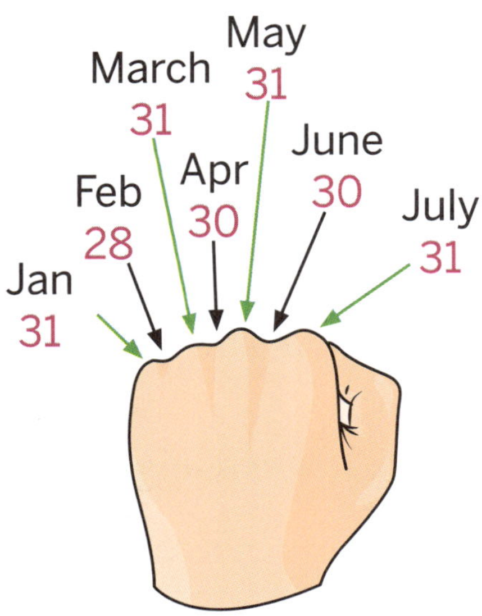

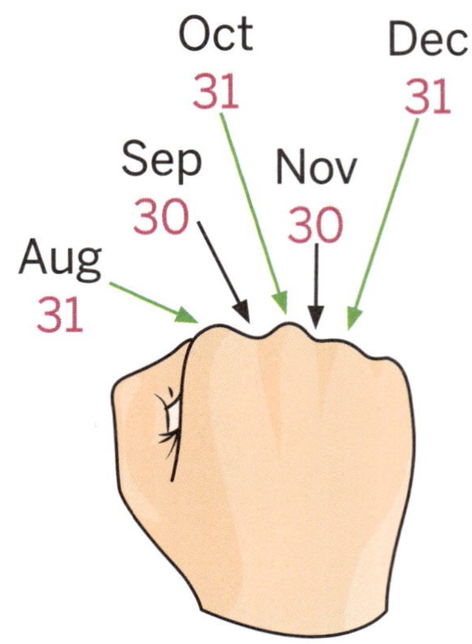

Start counting the months from the left. The knuckles jutting out are taken as the months with 31 days. The grooves (the parts between the knuckles) are taken to be the months with 30 days or Feb with 28 or 29 days.

Given below is the calendar of 2017 which shows the dates and the days of the months.

January

Su	Mo	Tu	We	Th	Fr	Sa
1	2	3	4	5	6	7
8	9	10	11	12	13	14
15	16	17	18	19	20	21
22	23	24	25	26	27	28
29	30	31				

February

Su	Mo	Tu	We	Th	Fr	Sa
			1	2	3	4
5	6	7	8	9	10	11
12	13	14	15	16	17	18
19	20	21	22	23	24	25
26	27	28				

March

Su	Mo	Tu	We	Th	Fr	Sa
			1	2	3	4
5	6	7	8	9	10	11
12	13	14	15	16	17	18
19	20	21	22	23	24	25
26	27	28	29	30	31	

April

Su	Mo	Tu	We	Th	Fr	Sa
						1
2	3	4	5	6	7	8
9	10	11	12	13	14	15
16	17	18	19	20	21	22
23	24	25	26	27	28	29
30						

May

Su	Mo	Tu	We	Th	Fr	Sa
	1	2	3	4	5	6
7	8	9	10	11	12	13
14	15	16	17	18	19	20
21	22	23	24	25	26	27
28	29	30	31			

June

Su	Mo	Tu	We	Th	Fr	Sa
				1	2	3
4	5	6	7	8	9	10
11	12	13	14	15	16	17
18	19	20	21	22	23	24
25	26	27	28	29	30	

July

Su	Mo	Tu	We	Th	Fr	Sa
						1
2	3	4	5	6	7	8
9	10	11	12	13	14	15
16	17	18	19	20	21	22
23	24	25	26	27	28	29
30	31					

August

Su	Mo	Tu	We	Th	Fr	Sa
		1	2	3	4	5
6	7	8	9	10	11	12
13	14	15	16	17	18	19
20	21	22	23	24	25	26
27	28	29	30	31		

September

Su	Mo	Tu	We	Th	Fr	Sa
					1	2
3	4	5	6	7	8	9
10	11	12	13	14	15	16
17	18	19	20	21	22	23
24	25	26	27	28	29	30

October

Su	Mo	Tu	We	Th	Fr	Sa
1	2	3	4	5	6	7
8	9	10	11	12	13	14
15	16	17	18	19	20	21
22	23	24	25	26	27	28
29	30	31				

November

Su	Mo	Tu	We	Th	Fr	Sa
			1	2	3	4
5	6	7	8	9	10	11
12	13	14	15	16	17	18
19	20	21	22	23	24	25
26	27	28	29	30		

December

Su	Mo	Tu	We	Th	Fr	Sa
					1	2
3	4	5	6	7	8	9
10	11	12	13	14	15	16
17	18	19	20	21	22	23
24	25	26	27	28	29	30
31						

Look at the calendar above. You will notice that February 1 is a Wednesday and March 21 is a Tuesday. A calendar helps us to find out the days and dates in a given year.

1. Look for your birthday in this calendar and find out what day it is.
2. Look for Republic Day, which is January 26, and find out what day it is.
3. Look for Independence Day, which is August 15, and find out what day it is.
4. Look for Christmas, which is December 25, and find out what day it is.

Try These!

In the calendar given, colour the months with 31 days red. How many are they?

Colour the months with 30 days green. How many are they? How many months have 28/29 days?

Exercise 10.4

1. Write the number of days in the following months.

a. January ___	b. February ___	c. March ___
d. April ___	e. May ___	f. June ___
g. July ___	h. August ___	i. September ___
j. October ___	k. November ___	l. December ___

2. How many months have 31 days? ____________
3. How many months have 30 days? ____________
4. Circle the month which has 28 or 29 days.

   January February March

5. Circle the months which have 31 days.

   May September June April July

6. Circle the months which have 30 days.

   February November August January May

7. Ankita's birth month has 30 days. Her birth month comes between January and May. What is Ankita's birth month?

Revision Exercise

1 Write the time shown in the following clocks. One has been done for you.

a.

5 o'clock

or

5:00

b.

____

or

____

c.

____

or

____

d.

____

or

____

e.

____

or

____

f.

____

or

____

g.

____

or

____

h.

____

or

____

i.

____

or

____

2 Draw the hands for the time given.

a. 

3 o'clock
or
3:00

b. 

5:15
or
Quarter past 5

c. 

Quarter to 11
or
10:45

d. 

7:30

e. 

10:10

f. 

4:40

3 Fill in the blanks.

a. The first day of the week is ________.

b. ________ and ________ make the weekend.

c. Wednesday comes after ________.

d. ________ comes after Monday.

4 If today is Wednesday, then

yesterday was ________.　　　　tomorrow will be ________.

5 Fill in the blanks.

a. January has ________ days.

b. September has ________ days.

6 Circle the months which have 31 days, tick the months which have 30 days and cross the month which has 28/29 days.

January	February	March	April	May	June
July	August	September	October	November	December

Worksheet

Write the timings of Sachin's day.

Sachin goes to school at ______ o'clock.

Each period at his school is for about 45 minutes.

Break starts at ______ and is for about 20 minutes.

His last class finishes at ______

He reaches home at ______ o'clock.

For the Curious Mind

February normally has 28 days.

Once every 4 years, we get an extra day which is put in the month of February as 29 February. That particular year is called a leap year.

Below is the list of a few years giving the number of days in February.

Year	2008	2009	2010	2011	2012	2013	2014	2015	2016
Number of days in February	29	28	28	28	29	28	28	28	29

Shapes

11

Shapes are formed out of lines and curves.

 is a line.  is a curve.

Let us revise some shapes we studied in Class 1.

Flat Shapes

Let us study more about flat shapes such as squares, rectangles, triangles, circles and ovals. They are also called plane shapes.

Sides and Corners

Some flat shapes are made of curved lines. And some flat shapes are made of straight lines. The shapes made with straight lines have corners. Corners are also called vertices.

Note

One corner will be called a vertex.

1. Square

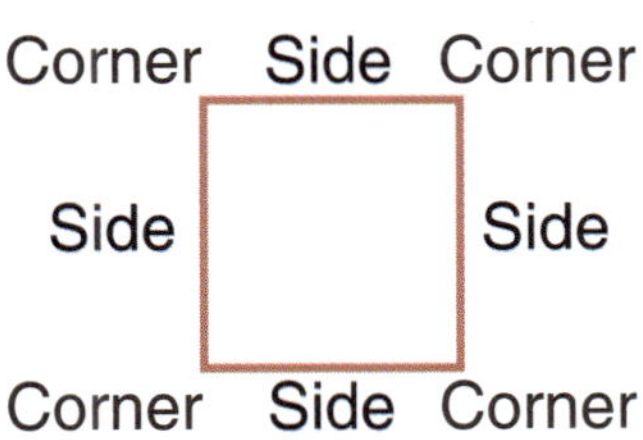

Number of sides = 4

Number of corners = 4

2. Rectangle

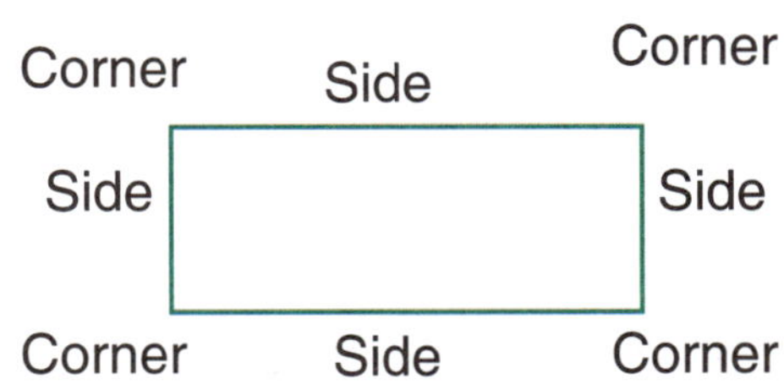

Number of sides = 4

Number of corners = 4

3. Triangle

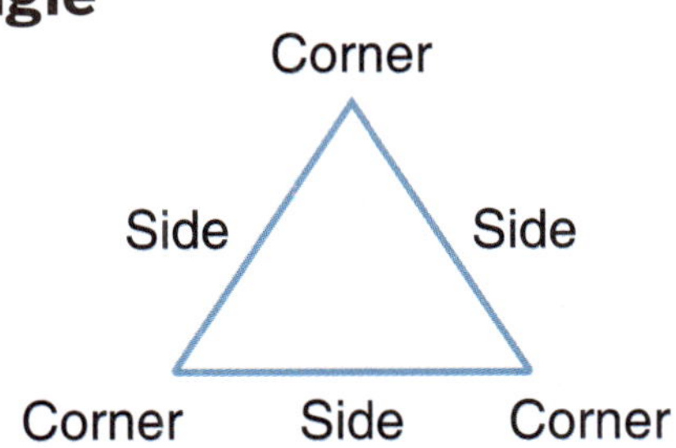

Number of sides = 3

Number of corners = 3

4. Circle

A circle is made up of a curve.

Number of sides = 0

Number of corners = 0

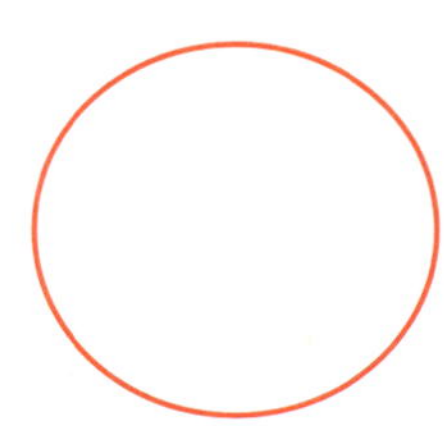

Solid Shapes

All the different shapes we see around us are solid shapes.

Let us study some solid shapes.

1. Cube

Number of corners = 8

Number of edges = 12

Number of faces = 6

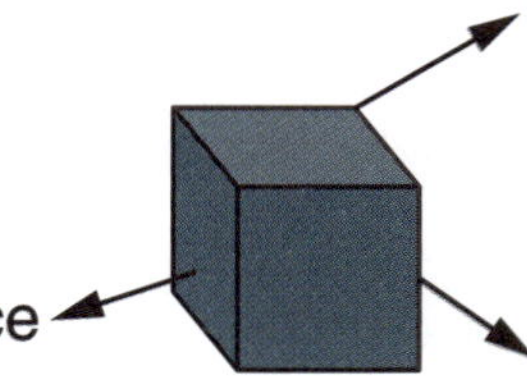

Note

All the faces of a cube and a cuboid are flat faces.

2. Cuboid

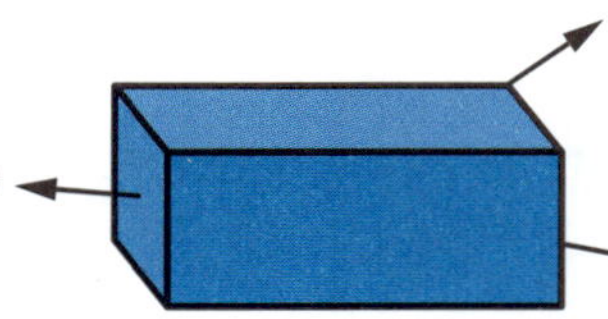

Number of corners = 8

Number of edges = 12

Number of faces = 6

Note

Some shapes like cube and cuboid have only flat faces. Some shapes like a sphere have only curved face. Some shapes like a cylinder and cone have both curved and flat faces.

3. Sphere

A sphere is like a marble.

Number of corners = 0

Number of edges = 0

Number of curved faces = 1

4. Cylinder

Number of curved faces = 1

Number of flat faces = 2

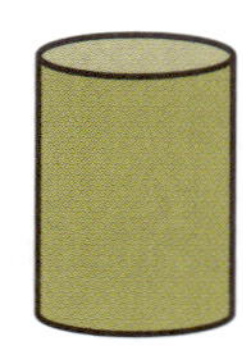

Note

The corner of a cone is different from the corner of a cube or cuboid. In a cone, the curved face meet at a point called the corner or apex.

5. Cone

Number of curved faces = 1

Number of flat faces = 1

Number of corners = 1

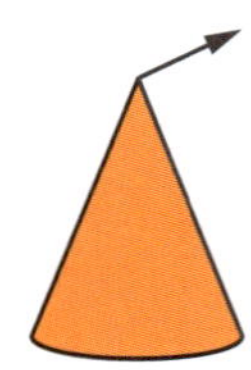

Rolling Objects and Sliding Objects

Objects that have curved faces can roll.

Objects that have flat faces can slide.

Objects that have both flat and curved faces can slide as well as roll.

Objects that can slide	Objects that can roll	Objects that can roll and slide

Exercise 11.1

Look at the shapes given below and answer the questions.

1. 

   Name of the shape = ________
   Number of corners = ________
   Number of sides = ________

2. 

   Name of the shape = ________
   Number of corners = ________
   Number of sides = ________

3. 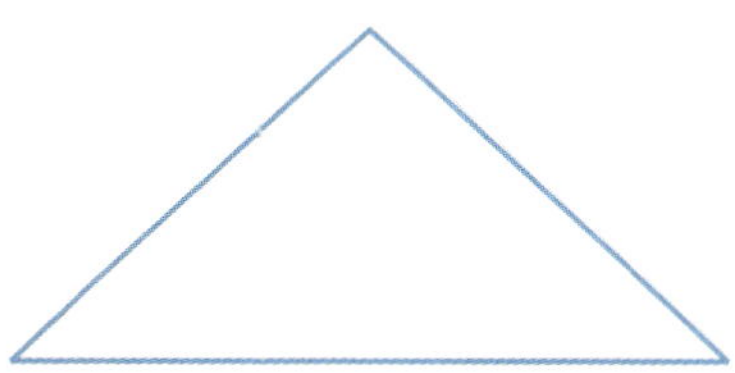

   Name of the shape = ________
   Number of corners = ________
   Number of sides = ________

4. 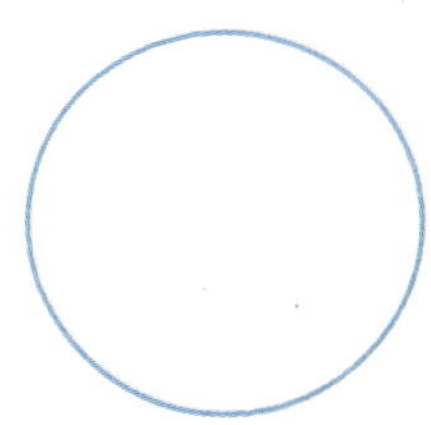

   Name of the shape = ________
   Number of corners = ________
   Number of sides = ________

5. 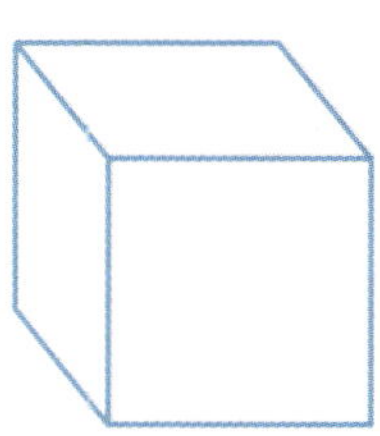

   Name of the shape = ________
   Number of corners = ________
   Number of edges = ________
   Number of faces = ________

6. 

   Name of the shape = ________
   Number of corners = ________
   Number of edges = ________
   Number of faces = ________

7

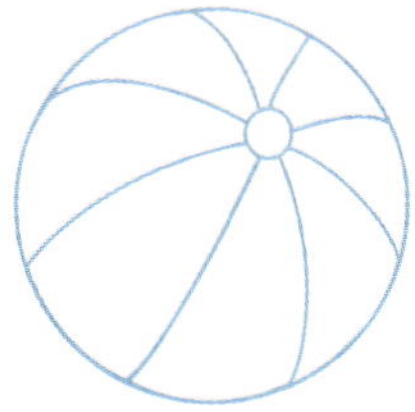

Name of the shape = ______

Number of corners = ______

Number of edges = ______

Number of faces = ______

8

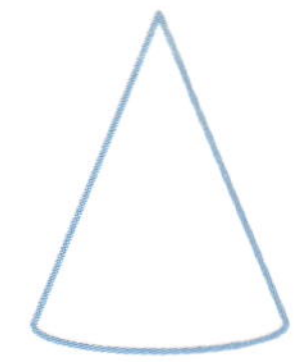

Name of the shape = ______

Number of corners = ______

Number of curved faces = ______

Number of flat faces = ______

9

Name of the shape = ______

Number of curved faces = ______

Number of flat faces = ______

Solid Shapes Around Us

Let us look at some examples of different solid shapes we see around us.

Objects that look like a cube

Objects that look like a cuboid

Objects that look like a sphere

Objects that look like a cylinder

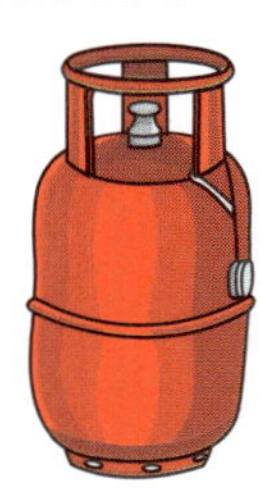

Objects that look like a cone

Exercise 11.2

Look at the objects shown below. Tick ☑ the shape each object reminds you of.

1. 

Sphere / Cuboid / Cone

2. 

Cube / Cone / Sphere

3. 

Cone / Sphere / Cube

4. 

Cylinder / Sphere / Cuboid

5. 

Cuboid / Cylinder / Sphere

6. 

Sphere / Cuboid / Cone

7. 

Cone / Cylinder / Cuboid

8. 

Cuboid / Cone / Cylinder

9. 

Cylinder / Cone / Cube

10. 

Cone / Cylinder / Sphere

11. 

Cylinder / Cone / Cube

12. 

Cylinder / Sphere / Cube

Revision Exercise

1 **Match the shapes in column A to their names in column B.**

A

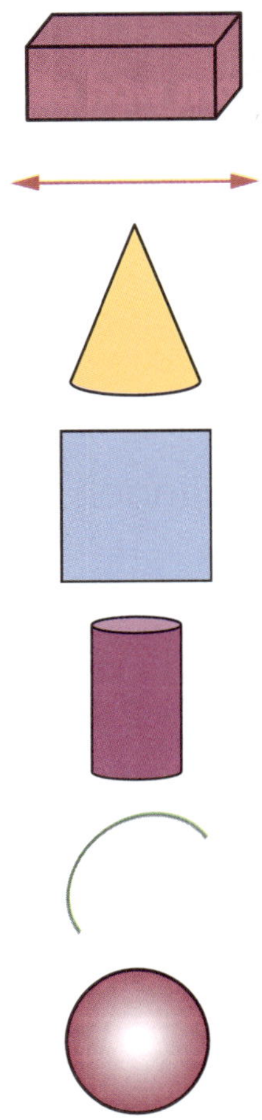

B

Line

Square

Cuboid

Cylinder

Cone

Sphere

Curve

2 **Write whether the following objects can roll (R), slide (S) or both (R and S). Write in the space provided.**

a.  ________

b.  ________

c. 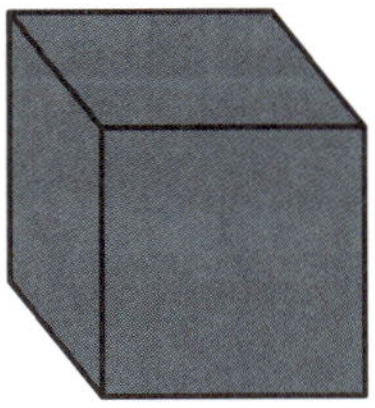 ________

d. 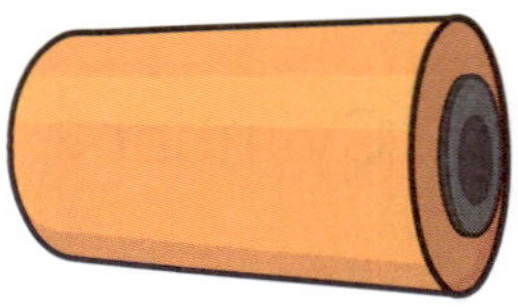 ________

Worksheet

Look at the given image and write the number of

a. triangles: ______

Colour them red.

b. circles: ______

Colour the small circles black and the big circle green.

c. cylinders: ______

Colour them blue.

d. rectangles: ______

Colour them yellow.

Mental Maths

Fill in the blanks.

1. A square has ____ sides and ____ corners.

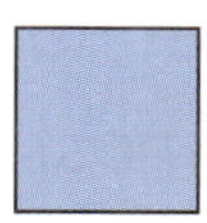

2. A circle has ____ corners.

3. A cube has ____ edges.

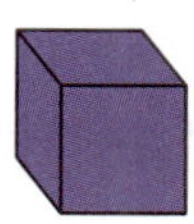

4. A cuboid has ____ faces.

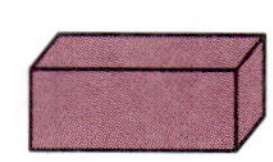

5. A sphere has ____ curved faces.

6. A cylinder has ____ flat circles.

7. A cone has ____ corner(s).

8. A rectangle has ____ sides.

9. A triangle has ____ sides.

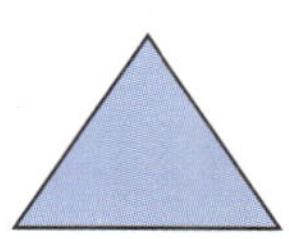

10. A cone has ____ flat circle(s).

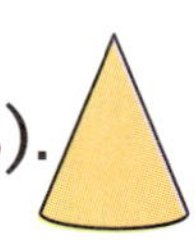

Data Handling

12

We observe and write facts about objects. This helps us to answer questions about those objects.

1. Raghav's collection of toy cars is shown below. Observe the pictures and answer the questions.

a. The number of red cars = 5

b. The number of yellow cars = 3

c. The number of green cars = 3

d. The number of blue cars = 4

e. The number of pink cars = 2

i. What is the total number of cars that Raghav has? 17

ii. Which colour car does he have the most? Red

iii. Which colour car does he have the least? Pink

iv. How many more red cars does he have than the blue cars? 1

v. Which cars does he have in equal number? Yellow and green

2. The following chart shows the number of cherries Anju ate during the week.

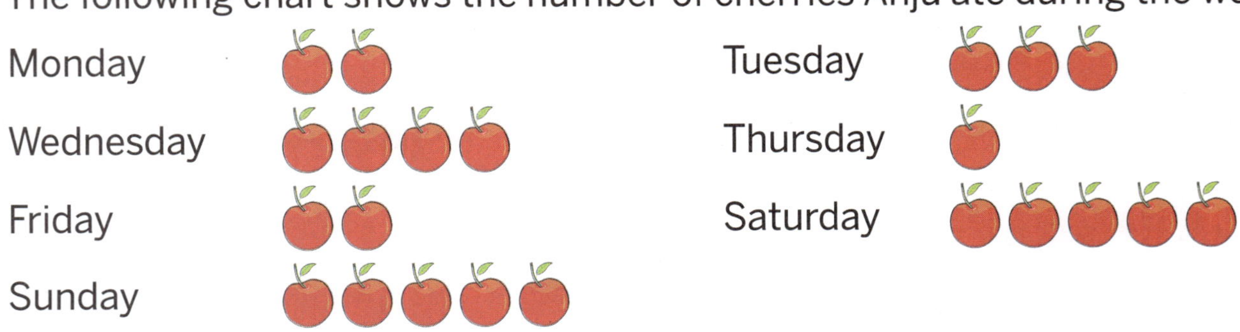

a. What is the total number of cherries Anju ate during the week?

Total number of cherries Anju ate = 2 + 3 + 4 + 1 + 2 + 5 + 5 = 22

b. How many cherries did she eat on Wednesday?

Number of cherries she ate on Wednesday = 4

c. On which day(s) did she eat 2 cherries?

She ate 2 cherries on Monday and Friday.

d. On which day did she eat the least number of cherries?

She ate the least number of cherries on Thursday.

e. Fill in the blanks.

i. She ate 2 cherries on Friday.

ii. She ate 5 cherries each on Saturday and Sunday.

iii. She ate 1 more cherry on Tuesday than Monday.

Exercise 12.1

Seema painted the following stars on her wall.

1. What is the number of

a. Pink stars? ______ b. blue stars? ______ c. Green stars? ______

d. Red stars? ______ e. Yellow stars? ______

2. What is the total number of stars she painted? ________
3. How many more pink stars does she have than blue stars? ________
4. In which colour did she paint the maximum number of stars? ________
5. In which two colors did she paint the least number of stars?
________ and ________
6. How many more green stars did she paint than blue stars? ________

Revision Exercise

1 Following are the number of tigers, elephants and giraffes in a zoo.

a. What is the number of tigers in the zoo? ______

b. What is the number of elephants in the zoo? ______

c. What is the number of giraffes in the zoo? ______

d. What is the total number of tigers, giraffes and elephants in the zoo? ______

e. How many more elephants are there than giraffes? ______

f. How many more elephants are there than tigers? ______

2 For the class party, the teacher bought

20 vanilla ice creams,
25 chocolate ice creams,
20 chocobars,
15 strawberry ice creams.

a. How many ice creams did the teacher buy in total? ______

b. How many more chocobars did the teacher buy than strawberry ice creams? ______

c. Which type ice cream did the teacher buy the most? ______

d. Which type ice cream did the teacher buy the least? ______

e. Which two ice creams did the teacher buy in the same number? ______

Mixed Review 3

1 **Match the money in column A to its value in column B.**

A	B
 + 	₹15
 + 	₹60
 + 	₹600
 + 	₹8
 +  + 	₹501
 + 	₹105

2 If toy car costs ₹243, how much will 3 toy cars cost?

1 car costs ______.

3 toy cars costs ______.

Thus, 3 toy cars will cost ₹ ______.

3 Distribute ₹225 among 9 people. How much will each person get?

Each person will get ₹ ______.

4 **Draw the hands in the clocks to show the time.**

a. 7 o'clock or 7:00

b. 9:30 or Half past 9

5. If today is Thursday, then

yesterday was ____________. tomorrow will be ____________.

6. Write the days of the week which come after

a. Tuesday ____________ b. Friday ____________ c. Sunday ____________

7. **Fill in the blanks.**

a. There are ______ months in a year. b. There are ______ days in a week.

c. December has ______ days. d. June has ______ days.

8. **Underline the appropriate unit of measurement for the following.**

a. 

length of the book
m, cm, g

b. 

height of the wall
m, ℓ, mℓ

c. 

weight of the chocolate
ℓ, g, m

d. 

weight of a child
cm, m, kg

e. 

amount of juice
kg, mℓ, cm

f. 

amount of water in a bucket
ℓ, g, kg

g. 

length of the table
g, ℓ, m

h. 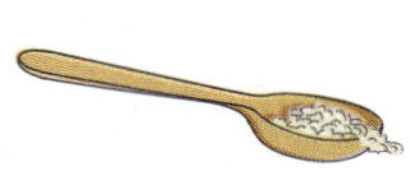

teaspoon of sugar
km, ℓ, g

i. 

basket of fruits
m, cm, kg

9 **Match the pictures in column A to their names in column B.**

A	B
	Square
	Circle
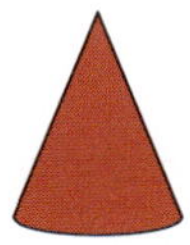	Cylinder
	Triangle
	Cone
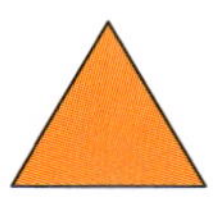	Cuboid
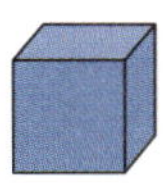	Rectangle
	Cube

10 **Following is the list of students who like to play different games in a class.**

Game	Number of children
Cricket	10
Basketball	12
Tennis	8

a. Which game is played by the most number of students? ________

b. Which game is played by the least number of students? ________

c. How many more students like to play basketball than cricket? ________

d. How many more students like to play basketball than tennis? ________

Test 1

1 **Fill in the blanks.**

a. 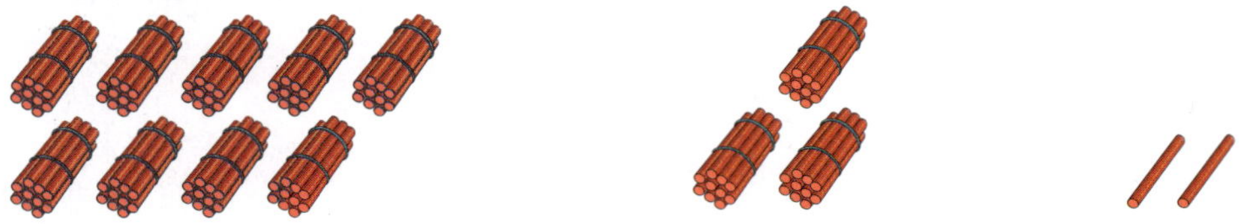

______ Hundreds   ______ Tens   ______ Ones

Number name: ______________________________

b. 482 = ______ hundreds ______ tens ______ ones

2 Write the numeral for nine hundred nine. ______

3 Write the four numbers that come after 352.

______, ______, ______, ______

4 In 925, the place value of 9 is ______ and the face value of 9 is ______.

5 **Write the following numbers in ascending order.**

792, 183, 567, 901

______, ______, ______, ______

6 **Fill in the blanks with >, < or =.**

a. 469 ______ 271   b. 682 ______ 893

7 **Fill in the blanks:**

3 + 5 = ______   30 + 50 = ______   300 + 500 = ______

8 **Add the following.**

a.

	H	T
	5	7
	2	3
+	1	2

b.

	H	T	O
	2	4	6
	5	0	3
+	1	1	2

9 A dealer sold 259 cars in March and 304 cars in April. How many cars did he sell in March and April?

		H	T	O
Cars sold in March				
Cars sold in April	+			
Total cars sold				

Thus, he sold _____ cars in March and April.

10 **Subtract the following.**

a. 350 – 0 = ____ b. 9 – 2 = ____ c. 90 – 20 = ____ d. 900 – 200 = ____

11 **Subtract the following.**

	H	T	O
	5	4	8
–	1	2	6

	H	T	O
	3	9	2
–		1	7

	H	T	O
	7	0	1
–		3	9

	H	T	O
	3	0	0
–		5	2

12 Out of 846 animals in a zoo, 19 fell sick on Monday. How many animals were not sick?

Total number of animals = ______

Number of sick animals = ________

Thus, ______ animals were not sick.

13 There were 25 flowers blooming in a garden. 12 more flowers bloomed in the morning. By evening, 7 flowers died. How many flowers were left in the garden?

Thus, _______ flowers were left.

14 If 1 box contains 5 chocolates, how many chocolates do 7 boxes contain?

Thus, 7 boxes contain _______ chocolates.

15 Distribute ₹ 240 among 8 people. How much will each person get?

Thus, each person will get _______.

16 Rajan bought a book for ₹ 350 and a mug for ₹ 75. How much more did the book cost than the mug?

Thus, the book cost _______ more than the mug.

17 **Write the time shown in the following clocks.**

a. 

________ or ________

b. 

________ or ________

c. 

________ or ________

d. 

________ or ________

18 April has ________ days and December has ________ days.

19 Circle the appropriate measurement for the following.

a. 

Length of the bus

kg m ℓ

b. 

Weight of the apples

mℓ cm kg

20 Colour the picture according to the colour code provided below.

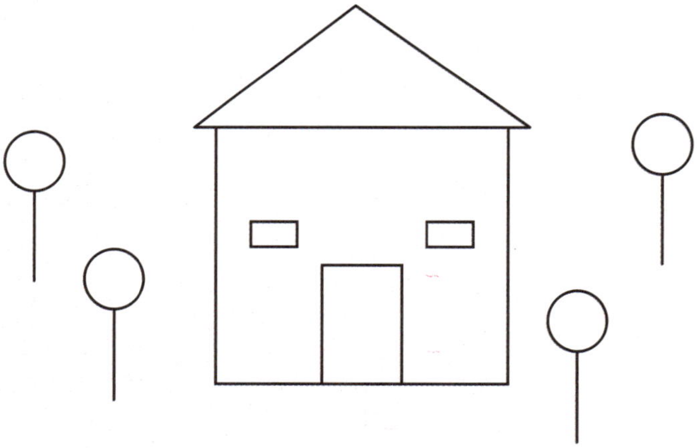

Colour the triangle red.
Colour the rectangle blue.

Colour the square yellow.
Colour the circles pink.

Test 2

1 Write the number name for

a. 596: ____________________

b. 907: ____________________

2 Fill in the blanks.

a. 297 = ________ hundreds ________ tens ________ ones

b. 861 = ________ hundreds ________ tens ________ one

3 In 725, the

a. place value of 7 is ________.   b. place value of 5 is ________.

4 Write the expanded from of 643. ____________________

5 Fill in the blanks with >, < or =.

a. 293 ________ 584   b. 900 ________ 899   c. 146 ________ 146

6 Write the following numbers in descending order.

521, 793, 964, 108

______, ______, ______, ______

7 Write the number that comes before the given number.

______, 799

8 Solve the following.

a.

	H	T	O
	1	2	6
	3	5	4
+	2	0	3

b.

	H	T	O
	2	6	7
	4	3	2
+	2	1	4

c.

	H	T	O
	4	7	5
+	4	5	8

d.

	H	T	O
	1	2	7
+	5	4	8

9 Solve the following.

a.

	H	T	O
	8	3	0
−	6	1	4

b.

	H	T	O
	7	0	3
−		2	9

c.

	H	T	O
	8	0	0
−		3	8

d.

	H	T	O
	7	8	9
−	3	7	5

10 **Solve the following.**

a.

H	T	O
4	1	3
×		2

b.

H	T	O
1	2	4
×		3

c.

H	T	O
1	3	8
×		4

11 **Solve the following.**

a. 360 ÷ 3　　b. 681 ÷ 3　　c. 306 ÷ 6

12 **A town has 673 cars and 105 bikes. How many cars and bikes are there in the town?**

Number of cars = ______

Number of bikes = ______

______

There are ______ cars and bikes in the town.

13 A school has 593 girls and 587 boys. How many more girls are there than boys?

Number of girls = ______

Number of boys = ______

______

There are ______ more girls than boys.

14 There are 25 children in Class 2. Each child brings 8 balloons for the class party. How many balloons will be collected for the class party?

______ balloons will be collected for the class party.

15 42 children were divided into 6 groups. How many children were there in each group?

There were ______ children in each group.

16 1 mug costs ₹ 13. How much will 5 mugs cost?

5 mugs will cost ______.

17 If 5th January is a Sunday, then

a. 6th January is a ____________.

b. 7th January is a ____________.

c. 8th January is a ____________.

18 **Tick yes or no for the following.**

a. Can 2 potatoes weigh 5 g? yes / no

b. Can a table be 1 metre long? yes / no

c. Can a glass contain 200 litres of water? yes / no

d. Can a bed be 3 cm long? yes / no

19 **Circle the appropriate measurement for the following.**

a. 

Weight of the bricks

m kg ℓ

b. 

Length of the mobile phone

km kg cm

20 **Fill in the blanks.**

a. A sphere has ______ corners and ______ sides.

b. A cube has ______ corners and ______ edges.

Answers

Chapter – 1

Exercise 1.1

1. a. 1 hundreds 2 tens 2 ones; one hundred twenty-two
   b. 2 hundreds 5 tens 1 ones; two hundred fifty-one
   c. 3 hundreds 1 tens 4 ones; three hundred fourteen
2. a. 2, 6, 5
   Two hundred sixty-five.
   b. 9, 3, 4
   Nine hundred thirty – four.
   c. 4,2, 8
   Four hundred twenty eight.
   d. 7,0, 3
   Seven hundred three.
3. a. 528 b. 713 c. 999 d. 287 e. 631 f. 164
4. a. 242, 243, 244, 245. b. 537, 538, 539, 540.
   c. 913, 914, 915, 916. d. 830, 831, 832, 833.
5. a. 247 b. 740 c. 550 d. 922.

Exercise 1.2

1. a. 432 b. 251 c. 407 d. 600
2. a.

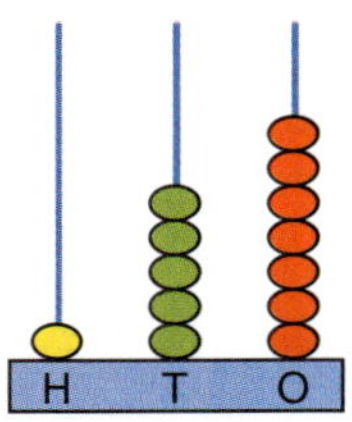

b.

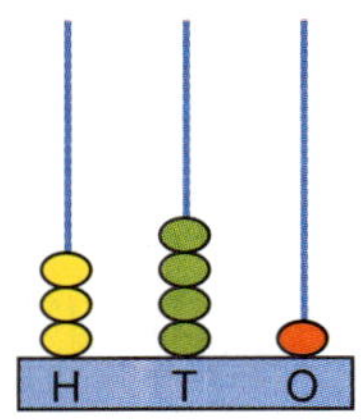

c.

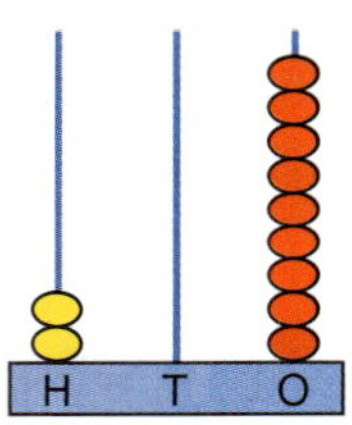

d.

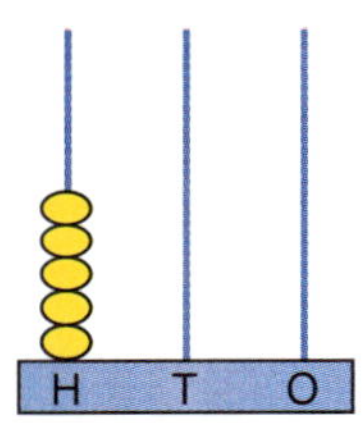

3. a.

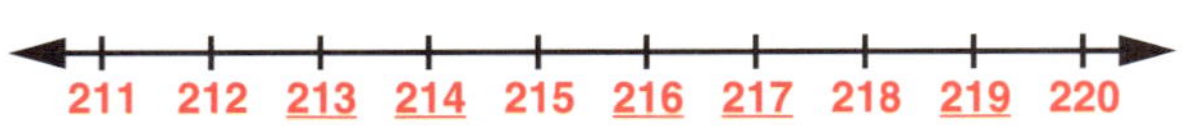

b.

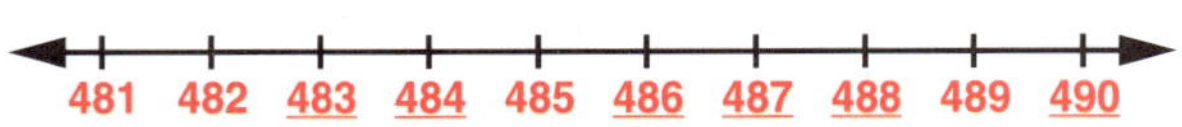

c.

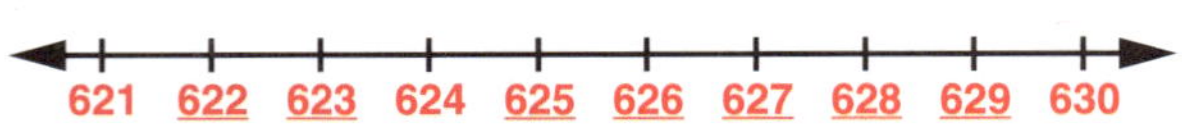

d.

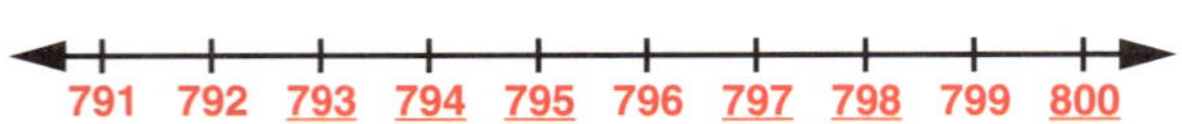

e.

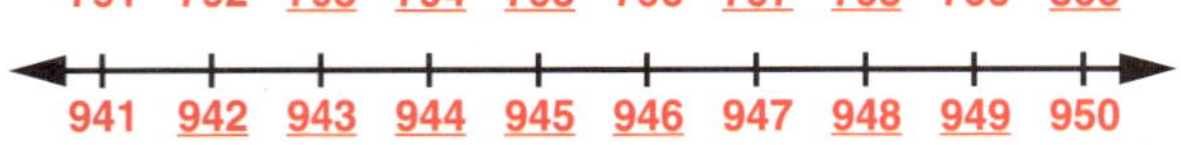

Exercise1.3

1. a. 2,7,1 ; 200 + 70 + 1. b. 5,8,3 ; 500 + 80 + 3.
   c. 4,9,6 ; 400 + 90 + 6.
2. a. Place value = 300, 40, 6.
   Face value = 3, 4, 6.
   b. Place value = 500, 60, 7.
   Face value = 5, 6, 7.
   c. Place value = 100, 80, 2.
   Face value = 1, 8, 2
   d. Place value = 400, 50, 3.
   Face value = 4, 5, 3
3. a. 400 b. 70 c. 9 d. 40
4. a. 5 b. 3 c. 1 d. 4.

Exercise 1. 4

1. a. > b. > c. <, d. = e. < f. =
   g. < h. < i. > j. < k. < l. >
2. a. 539 b. 890 c. 918 d. 851
3. a. 198 b. 349 c. 215 d. 159

Exercise 1.5

1. a. 104, 350, 692, 793. b. 273, 341, 512, 860.
   c. 470, 695, 721, 900. d. 163, 409, 532, 817.
2. a. 893, 781, 529, 234. b. 804, 712, 659, 237.
   c. 999, 618, 493, 270. d. 739, 527, 200, 168.
3. a. 340, 350, 360, 370. b. 560, 570, 580, 590.
   c. 630, 640, 650, 660. d. 880, 890, 900, 910.
   e. 760, 770, 780, 790. f. 420, 430, 440, 450.
4. a. 960, 950, 940, 930. b. 740, 730, 720, 710.
   c. 250, 240, 230, 220. d. 420, 410, 400, 390.
   e. 830, 820, 810, 800. f. 370, 360, 350, 340.

Exercise 1.6

1. a. 206 b. 725 c. 598 d. 862 e. 614 f. 287
   g. 940 h. 751 i. 143
2. a. 634 b. 497 c. 922 d. 716 e. 187 f. 549
   g. 288 h. 829 i. 340.
3. a. 168 b. 824 c. 981 d. 770
   e. 211,212 f. 544,545 g. 630,631 h. 170, 171
   i. 400,401 j. 667, 668.

Revision Exercise

1. a. 2, 9, 9 ; Two hundred ninety-nine
   b. 1, 6, 1; One hundred sixty-one
2. a. 4, 2, 9
   Four hundred twenty – nine.
   b. 9, 7, 8
   Nine hundred seventy – eight.
3. a. 506 b. 999
4. 624, 625, 626, 627 ;
   863, 864, 865, 866.
5. a. 625
   b.

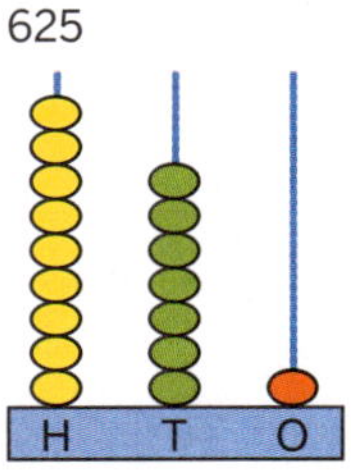

6. a.

   b. 9, 3, 5 ; 900 + 30 + 5. c. 600; 6.
7. a. > b. > c. < d. =
8. 192, 529, 684, 983.
9. 963, 814, 571, 248.
10. a. 450, 460, 470.
   b.

11. a. 734 b. 284 c. 949

Worksheet

1. a. 5, 9, 3. b. 7, 8, 1
2. a. 4 b. 7
3. a. (782) 196 × b. (965) 106 × c. (648) 235 ×
4. a. < b. < c. < d. =
5. a. 899 b. 679 c. 692

For The Curious Mind !!

1. 183 2. 355 3. 940 4. 500 5. 710

Chapter – 2

Exercise 2.1

1. a. 5 b. 46 c. 871 d. 396
2. a. 3, 30, 300. b. 8, 80, 800.
   c. 9, 90, 900. d. 5, 50, 500.
3. a. 797 b. 979 c. 678 d. 878 e. 498
   f. 197 g. 988 h. 586 i. 898 j. 720
   k. 390 l. 540 m. 689 n. 569 o. 789

Exercise 2.2

1. a. 876 b. 779 c. 897 d. 989 e. 799
   f. 999 g. 899 h. 968 i. 966 j. 789
   k. 898 l. 698 m. 958 n. 868 o. 700

Exercise 2.3

1. a. 86 b. 98 c. 89 d. 78 e. 97
   f. 98 g. 87 h. 67 i. 79
2. a. 578 b. 987 c. 678 d. 868 e. 799
   f. 696 g. 600 h. 800 i. 900 j. 978
   k. 896 l. 865

Exercise 2.4

1. a. 686 b. 751 c. 864 d. 966 e. 972
   f. 886 g. 795 h. 893 i. 688 j. 594
   k. 586 l. 894

Exercise 2.5

1. a. 744 b. 966 c. 933 d. 954 e. 957
   f. 851 g. 963 h. 823 i. 817 j. 853
   k. 797 l. 953 m. 856 n. 749 o. 757

Exercise 2.6

1. 588 2. 730 3. 157 4. 425 5. 835
6. 887 7. 568 8. 450

Revision Exercise

1. a. 4, 40, 400. b. 7, 70, 700.
2. a. 868 b. 599 c. 800 d. 88 e. 93
   f. 898 g. 600 h. 871 i. 923 j. 854
   k. 880 l. 777

3. $\begin{array}{r} 2\,3\,5 \\ +\,2\,4\,5 \\ \hline 4\,8\,0 \end{array}$ 4. $\begin{array}{r} 4\,5\,7 \\ +\,4\,6\,3 \\ \hline 9\,2\,0 \end{array}$ 5. $\begin{array}{r} 2\,5\,6 \\ 2\,2\,8 \\ +\,1\,2\,6 \\ \hline 6\,1\,0 \end{array}$

Worksheet

1. a.

+	80	60	90	70
253	333	313	343	323
185	265	245	275	255
693	773	753	783	763

b.

+	245	338	152	227
135	380	473	287	362
226	471	564	378	543
641	886	979	793	868

2. a. 600 b. 400 & 500 c. 200 & 400.
3. 665 gram.

For The Curious Mind !!

870 Km.

Chapter – 3

Exercise 3.1

1. a. 9 b. 53 c. 384 d. 721
2. a. 612 b. 841 c. 252 d. 575 e. 323 f. 331
   g. 122 h. 343 i. 541 j. 422 k. 321 l. 671
   m. 231 n. 231 o. 923 p. 813

Exercise 3.2

1. a. 331 b. 471 c. 772 d. 100 e. 541 f. 163
   g. 321 h. 200 i. 131 j. 143 k. 321 l. 400
   m. 251 n. 322 o. 241 p. 222

Exercise 3.3

1. a. 727 b. 917 c. 859 d. 369 e. 627 f. 259
   g. 544 h. 159 i. 264 j. 188 k. 437 l. 358
   m. 478 n. 598 o. 783 p. 418.

Exercise 3.4

1. a. 107 b. 404 c. 319 d. 88 e. 342 f. 219
   g. 416 h. 528 i. 158 j. 428 k. 578 l. 169
   m. 348 n. 469 o. 174 p. 159.
2. a. 46 b. 224 c. 218 d. 407 e. 132 f. 326
   g. 543 h. 78 i. 109 j. 168 k. 153 l. 171
3. a. 115 b. 359 c. 459 d. 179 e. 477 f. 738
   g. 468 h. 257 i. 514 j. 466 k. 308 l. 65

Exercise 3.5

1. 875 2. 862 3. 26 4. 868
5. 137 ice creams. 6. 21 7. 121
8. 235 9. 225 10. 11 chocolates

Exercise 3.6

1. 429 2. 164 3. 590 4. 2 5. 438
6. 140 7. 498

Revision Exercise

1. a. 1, 10, 100. b. 4, 40, 400. c. 3, 30, 300.
2. a. 512 b. 519 c. 483 d. 247 e. 711 f. 557
   g. 779 h. 464 i. 542 j. 633 k. 359 l. 853
3. 48 4. ₹890

Worksheet

1. a. 45 cm b. 35 cm c. 55 cm d. 15 cm e. 25 cm

Mental Maths

1. 187 2. 900 3. 300

For The Curious Mind !!

110 students.

Chapter – 4

Let's Get Started

1. a. 14 b. 9 c. 0 d. 20
   e. 50 f. 0

Exercise 4.1

1. a. 6, 3 ; $3 \times 6 = 18$. b. 3, 4 ; $4 \times 3 = 12$.
2. a. 4×3 b. 6×7 c. 7×2
3. a. 7×2 b. 4×6 c. 5×9 d. 3×10

Exercise 4.2

1. a. 3, 5, 15 b. 4, 2, 8. c. 10,5,50 d. 25, 1, 25
2. a. 3 b. 6 c. 3 d. 55
3. a. 3 b. 5 c. 10 d. 7
4. a. 0 b. 0 c. 0 d. 0

Exercise 4.3

2. a. 12 b. 6 c. 20 d. 35 e. 18 f. 28
   g. 48 h. 18 i. 30 j. 14 k. 24 l. 36
   m. 30 n. 56 o. 63
3. a. 6 b. 20 c. 7 d. 12 e. 30 f. 21

Exercise 4.4

1. a. 69 b. 67 c. 36 d. 79 e. 96 f. 80
   g. 63 h. 90 i. 98 j. 639 k. 208 l. 978
   m. 408 n. 693 o. 600

Exercise 4.5

1. a. 60 b. 144 c. 438 d. 150 e. 215 f. 94
 g. 135 h. 588 i. 222 j. 574 k. 84 l. 310
 m. 736 n. 138 o. 190
2. a. 980 b. 918 c. 822 d. 858 e. 730 f. 512
 g. 981 h. 940 i. 918 j. 852 k. 795 l. 456
 m. 717 n. 992 o. 716

Exercise 4.6

1. 3; 7 × 3 ; 21. 2. 24 3. 32 4. 20
5. 42 6. 28

Exercise 4.7

1. 159 people 2. 296 3. 750 4. 560 5. 378

For The Curious Mind !!

8000 ; 80000

Revision Exercise

1. 2, 9, 18
2. a. 6 b. 4 c. 9 d. 0
3. a. 15 b. 48 c. 27 d. 12 e. 28 f. 24
4. a. 60 b. 300 c. 800
5. a. 26 b. 204 c. 246 d. 968.
6. 35 7. 525.

Mixed Review 1

1. a. 1,5, 3; One hundred fifty-three
2. a. 8, 8, 9 ; Eight hundred eighty – nine.
 b. 1, 4, 8 ; One hundred forty – eight.
3. a. < b. <
4. 6, 60, 600
5. a. 787 b. 440 c. 800 d. 67 e. 75 f. 896
6. a. 5, 50, 500.
7. a. 131 b. 934 c. 431 d. 338.
8. a. 28 b. 24 c. 18 d. 30 e. 80 f. 350
 g. 600 h. 700 i. 800
9. 6, 60, 600.
10. a. 48 b. 100 c. 963 d. 375 e. 835
11. 132 12. 36 13. 118 14. ₹225
15. 750 16. 980

Chapter – 5

Exercise 5.1

1. a. 4, 3 b. 3, 6 c. 4, 7 d. 9, 8 e. 7, 5 f. 9, 2
2. a. 14 b. 36 c. 63 d. 24
3. a. 2 b. 3 c. 10 d. 4

Exercise 5.2

3. 2 4. 6 5. 8 6. 3 7. 9
8. 5 9. 2 10. 7

Exercise 5.3

1. 3. 2. 5 3. 5 4. 2 5. 4
6. 2 7. 6 8. 4 9. 6

Exercise 5.4

1. Q = 2, R = 1. 2. Q = 1, R = 5.
3. Q = 4, R = 1. 4. Q = 3, R =3.
5. Q = 1, R = 3. 6. Q = 4, R = 3.
7. Q = 3, R = 3. 8. Q = 6, R = 1.
9. Q= 3, R= 5.

Exercise 5.5

1. Q = 32, R = 0. 2. Q = 15, R = 1.
3. Q = 12, R = 2. 4. Q = 12, R = 5.
5. Q = 12, R = 0. 6. Q = 11, R = 5.
7. Q = 31, R = 0. 8. Q = 17, R = 0.
9. Q = 10, R = 0. 10. Q = 16, R = 3.
11. Q = 14, R = 2. 12. Q = 13, R = 3.
13. Q = 13, R = 2. 14. Q = 12, R = 3.
15. Q = 9, R = 5.

Revision Exercise

1. a. 6, 5 b. 3, 7.
2. a. 28 b. 27
3. a. 2 b. 4
4. a. Q = 4 b. Q = 9
5. a. Q = 6 b. Q = 5

2) 12 (6
 −12
 0

5) 25 (5
 −25
 0

 c. Q = 3 d. Q = 4
6. a. Q = 3, R = 1 b. Q = 3, R = 3
 c. Q = 1, R = 2 d. Q = 2, R = 5
7. a. Q = 28, R = 0 b. Q = 33, R = 0
 c. Q = 15, R = 3 d. Q = 12, R = 5
 e. Q = 49, R = 1 f. Q = 5, R = 6
 g. Q = 13, R = 1 h. Q = 10, R = 0

Worksheet

1. 36 → 7, 5
 7 × 5 = 35
 5 × 7 = 35
 35 ÷ 7 = 5
 35 ÷ 5 = 7

 36 → 9, 4
 9 × 4 = 36
 4 × 9 = 36
 36 ÷ 9 = 4
 36 ÷ 4 = 9
2. 78 ÷ 5 ___ 3 61 ÷ 3 ___ 1 84 ÷ 4 ___ No Remainder
 86 ÷ 9 ___ 5 92 ÷ 8 ___ 4 74 ÷ 6 ___ 2

For The Curious Mind !!

30 ÷ 5 = 6 50 ÷ 5 = 10 40 ÷ 2 = 20
50 ÷ 10 = 5 40 ÷ 4 = 10

Chapter – 6

Exercise 6.1

1. Q = 210, R = 2 2. Q = 123, R = 0
3. Q = 122, R = 0. 4. Q = 61, R = 0.
5. Q = 150, R = 2. 6. Q = 110, R = 4
7. Q = 102, R = 0. 8. Q = 310, R = 0.
9. Q = 122, R = 0. 10. Q = 121, R = 3.
11. Q = 115, R = 3. 12. Q = 71, R = 0.

Exercise 6.2

1. 24 ; 6 ; 4 2. 12 3. 2
4. 7 children, 2 left. 5. 2 6. 19
7. 50 8. 146 9. 12 children, 1 left.

Revision Exercise

1. a. Q = 22, R = 0. b. Q = 110, R = 0.
 c. Q = 51, R = 0 d. Q = 100, R = 0.
2. 81 3. 13 books, 2 left over. 4. 17

Worksheet

1. 19, 44, 101, 300 13, 21, 140, 110.
2. a. 24 bicycles b. 18 cars
 c. 14 buses, 1 tyre will be left. d. 5 piles, 5 tyres left over.

For the Curious Mind

10,2

Chapter – 7

Exercise 7.1

1. a. $\frac{1}{2}$ b. $\frac{1}{3}$ c. $\frac{1}{4}$
2. a. $\frac{1}{3}$ b. $\frac{1}{4}$

Revision Exercise

1. i) c   ii) a   iii) b

Mixed Review 2

1. 5 ; 7
2. a. Ans : 9, 9.   b. Ans : 7, 7.
   c. Ans : 8, 8.   d. Ans : 4, 4.
3. a. Q = 45, R = 0.   b. Q = 110, R = 0
   c. Q = 52, R = 0.   d. Q = 100, R = C
4. 14   5. 13 ; 2
6. a. 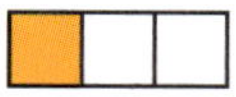   b. 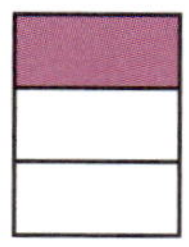   c. 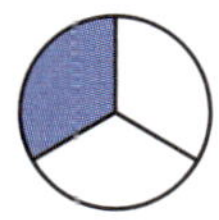
7. a.    b.    c. 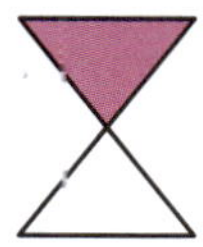

Chapter – 8

Exercise 8.1

1. Metre
2. Height of cup, length of a book, Length of a pencil.
3. length of a pencil, length of a T.V, length of an eraser.
4. a. cm   b. m   c. cm   d. cm   e. m   f. m

Try These !!

i. 300   ii. 900   iii. 8 m   iv. 7 m

Exercise 8.2

2. a. 2 cm   b. 3 cm   c. 4 cm   d. 5 cm
3. a. 700   b. 300   c. 600   d. 900
4. a. 8 ; 8   b. 4 × 100 = 4
   c. 7 × 100 = 7   d. 10 × 100 = 10

Exercise 8.3

1. a. 78 m 59 cm   b. 69 m 02 cm   c. 64 m 21 cm
   d. 64 m 25 cm   e. 98 m 67 cm   f. 43 m 40 cm
2. a. 43 m 32 cm   b. 43 m 66 cm   c. 25 m 88 cm
   d. 20 m 38 cm   e. 11 m 76 cm   f. 35 m 12 cm
3. a. 62 m 13 cm   b. 22 m 39 cm
4. a. 78 m 7 cm   b. 6 m 42 cm
5. 4 m 45 cm   6. 3 m 80 cm   7. 1 m 80 cm

Exercise 8.4

1. 500 g ;   2 Kg ;   15 g ;   1 Kg ;   10 g.
3. a. 1 kg   b. 500 g   c. 250 g   d. 100 g
   e. 5 g   f. 10 g

Exercise 8.5

1. a. 47 Kg 558 g   b. 62 Kg 847 g   c. 42 Kg 923 g
   d. 53 Kg 764 g   e. 63 Kg 758 g   f. 75 Kg 348 g
2. a. 3 Kg 763 g   b. 5 Kg 586 g   c. 3 Kg 560 g
   d. 21 Kg 259 g   e. 15 Kg 653 g   f. 15 Kg 445 g
3. a. 42 Kg 537 g   b. 56 Kg 185 g
   c. 15 Kg 28 g   d. 37 Kg 189 g
4. a. 41 Kg 153 g   b. 30 Kg 478 g
   c. 27 Kg 173 g   d. 48 Kg 977 g
5. a. 35 Kg 425 g
6. a. Gautam ; 10 Kg 760 g
7. 620 g.

Exercise 8.6

1. 5 ml ;   15 l ;   200 ml.   750 ml ;   1 ml ;   250 ml.

Exercise 8.7

1. a. 85 l 588 ml   b. 53 l 992 ml   c. 76 l 296 ml
   d. 52 l 027 ml   e. 92 l 254 ml   f. 20 l 570 ml
2. a. 5 l 564 ml   b. 6 l 068 ml   b. 17 l 180 ml
   d. 31 l 295 ml   e. 12 l 817 ml   f. 14 l 415 ml
3. a. 47 l 022 ml   b. 31 l 590 ml
   c. 7 l 31 ml   d. 17 l 230 ml
4. a. 31 l 251 ml   b. 33 l 484 ml
   c 19 l 389 ml   d. 17 l 979 ml
5. 31 l   6. 8 l 875 ml   7. 1 l 350 ml

Revision Exercise

1. a. 2 m   b. 7 cm
2. a. 200 g   b. 70 Kg
3. a. 250 ml   b. 5 l
4. 10 Km 240 m
5. Basket of flowers ; 325 g.
6. Tub ; 5 l 700 ml

Worksheet

1. 450 m   2. 125 m   3. Vijay's house   4. 575 m
5. 350 m   6. (a) -longest (b) - smallest

Chapter – 9

Exercise 9.1

1. a. 60   b. 72   c. 150   d. 201   e. 600   f. 21
2. a. <   b. >   c. =   d. >   e. =

Exercise 9.2

1. 940   2. 225   3. 55 ; 55 × 7 ; 385.
4. 324 ; 6 ; 54.   5. 581   6. 36   7. 5   8. 540
9. 49   10. 100   11. 360

Revision Exercise

1. a. <   b. =   c. >   d. >   e. =
2. a. 700   b. 300   c. 21   d. 16   e. 60
   f. 200   g. 600
3. a. 925, 750, 175.   4. 350, 1400   5. 755, 5, 151
6. 275, 650, 925   7. ₹25

Worksheet

1. ₹220 ;   ₹48 ;   ₹20 ; ₹100 ;   ₹292 ;   ₹478
2.

Cost/Item	Price	Correct amount
350	380	350
30	40	90
400	1200	1200
780	1620	1640

Mental maths

1. ₹80   2. ₹5 is left ; ₹95 more.

Chapter – 10

Exercise 10.1

1. a. 1 o'clock or 1 : 00   b. 7 o'clock or 7 : 00
   c. 11 o'clock or 11 : 00   d. 6 o'clock or 6 : 00.
2. 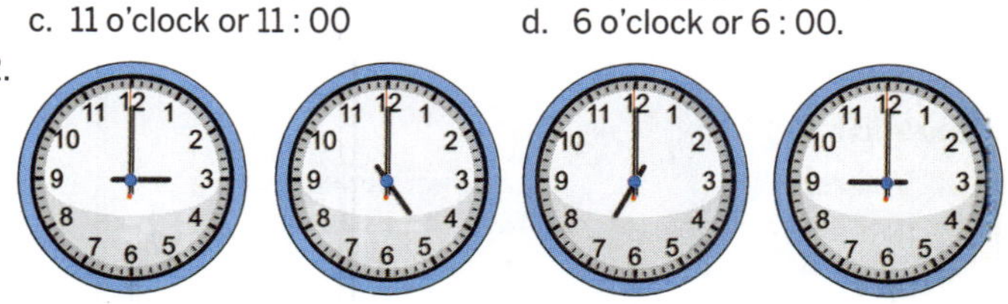

Exercise 10.2

a. 11 : 30 or half past 11   b. 3 : 30 or half past 3
c. 7 : 30 or half past 7   d. 1 : 30 or half past 1
e. 9 : 15 or quarter past 9   f. 5 : 15 or quarter past 5
g. 6 : 45 or quarter to 7   h. 10 : 45 or quarter to 11.

2.

Exercise 10.3

1. a. 7 b. Monday c. Thursday d. Wednesday
2. a. Monday, Wednesday 3. Thursday, Saturday
4. Saturday, Monday 5. Tuesday, Thursday
6. Friday, Sunday

Exercise 10.4

1. a. 31 b. 28 c. 31 d. 30 e. 31 f. 30
g. 31 h. 31 i. 30 j. 31 k. 30 l. 31
2. 7 3. 4 4. February 5. July, May
6. November 7. April

Revision Exercise

1. b. 9 o'clock or 9 : 00 c. 7 o'clock or 7 : 00
d. 9 : 15 or quarter past 9 e. 10 : 45 or quarter to 11.
f. 3 : 45 or quarter to 4. g. 8 : 10 or ten past 8.
h. 11 : 25 or twenty five minutes past 11.
i. 1 : 40 or forty minutes past 1.

2.

3. a. Monday b. Saturday and Sunday
c. Tuesday d. Tuesday 4. Tuesday, Thursday
5. a. 31 b. 30
6. January February March
April May June
July August September
October November December

Worksheet

8, 11: 30, 1 : 30, 2

Chapter – 11

Exercise 11.1

1. Square ; 4 ; 4 2. Rectangle ; 4 ; 4.
3. Triangle ; 3; 3 4. Circle ; 0, 0
5. Cube ; 8 ; 12 ; 6 6. Cuboid ; 8 ; 12; 6
7. Sphere ; 0 ; 0 ; 1 curved face.
8. Cone ; 1; 1 ; 1 9. Cylinder ; 1; 2.

Exercise 11.2

1. Cuboid 2. Cone 3. Cube 4. Cylinder
5. Sphere 6. Cuboid 7. Cuboid 8. Cone
9. Cylinder 10. Cylinder 11. Cube 12. Sphere

Revision Exercise

1. 1. Cuboid 2. Line 3. Cone 4. Square
5. Cylinder 6. Curve 7. Sphere
2. a. R and S b. R c. S d. R

Worksheet

a. 1 b. 9 c. 3 d. 3

Chapter – 12

Exercise 12.1

1. a. 5 b. 3 c. 4 d. 1 e. 1
2. 14 3. 2 4. Pink 5. Red and yellow 6. 1

Revision Exercise

1. a. 4 b. 6 c. 2 d. 12 e. 4 f. 2
2. a. 80 b. 5 c. Chocolate ice-cream
d. Strawberry ice-cream
e. Vanilla ice cream and chocobars.

Mixed Review 3

1. a. ₹600 b. ₹15 c. ₹60 d. ₹105 e. ₹8 f. ₹501
2. ₹243 ; ₹729 ; ₹729
3. 25
4. a.

b.

5. Wednesday ; Friday
6. a. Wednesday b. Saturday c. Monday
7. a. 12 b. 7 c. 31 d. 30
8. a. cm b. m c. g d. Kg e. ml f. l
g. m h. mg i. Kg
9. a. Cylinder b. Square c. Cone d. Circle
e. Rectangle f. Triangle g. Cube h. Cuboid
10. a. Basketball b. Tennis c. 2 d. 4

Test 1

1. a. 9 ; 3 ; 2 ; Nine hundred thirty – two. b. 4 ; 8; 2
2. 909 3. 353 ; 354 ; 355 ; 356.
4. 900 ; 9 5. 183 ; 567 ; 792 ; 901
6. a. > b. < 7. 8 ; 80 ; 800
8. a. 92 b. 861
9. 259 ; 304 ; 563 10. 350 ; 7 ; 70 ; 700.
11. 422 ; 375 ; 662 ; 248 12. 846 ; 19 ; 827.
13. 30 14. 35 15. ₹30 16. ₹275
17. a. 7 o'clock or 7 : 00 b. 5 : 30 or half past 5
c. 3 : 15 or quarter past 3 d. 4 : 45 or quarter to 5.
18. 30 ; 31
19. a. m b. Kg

Test 2

1. a. Five hundred ninety six. b. Nine hundred seven
2. a. 2 ; 9 ; 7 b. 8 ; 6 ; 1 3. 700 ; 5 4. 600 + 40 + 3
5. a. < b. > c. =
6. 964, 793, 521, 108.
7. 798
8. a. 683 b. 913 c. 933 d. 675
9. a. 216 b. 674 c. 762 d. 414
10. a. 826 b. 372 c. 552
11. a. 120 b. 227 c. 51
12. 673 ; 105 ; 778 13. 593 ; 587 ; 6
14. 200 15. 7 16. 65
17. a. Monday b. Tuesday c. Wednesday
18. a. No b. Yes c. No d. No
19. a. Kg b. cm
20. a. no ; no b. 8 ; 12.

Notes

Notes